Truth is Two-Eyed

JOHN A. T. ROBINSON

Truth is Two-Eyed

SCM PRESS LTD

334 01690 8

First published 1979
by SCM Press Ltd
58 Bloomsbury Street, London

Photoset by Input Typesetting Ltd
and printed in Great Britain by
Richard Clay Ltd,
Bungay, Suffolk

Contents

half months going round the world – a month in South Africa,
a month in Israel, a week in Iran, two months in India and
Sri Lanka, a fortnight in Hong Kong and Japan, and two
months in North America. I gave the Teape Lectures proper
in Delhi, Madras and Calcutta, and used much of the same
material for the Otis Lectures at Wheaton College, Massa-
chusetts. But at many other centres also we received so much
more than we gave, and we shall ever remain grateful for the
opening up of what was to us a new world. I am greatly
indebted to the Teape Lectureship trustees for their help and
encouragement and to those who arranged our programme
and entertained us so generously.

My hesitation in accepting the invitation to give the lectures
was matched only by my hesitation in deciding what to do
with them afterwards. My natural inclination was to feel that
there was nothing I could say which would justify inflicting
yet another book. But encouragement from friends and con-
sultants, a sense of obligation to those who did me the honour
of inviting me, and above all a conviction that I should at
least try to share with others what had stretched me, kept me
to it when the strong temptation was to concentrate on fields
in which I felt more at home. For I cannot presume to offer
anything here in the way of original learning. It is frustrating
to feel that one is constantly dependent on a language one
does not know, and, if only to save the printers trouble, I
have anglicized the Sanskrit and omitted the diacritical marks
in a manner that I hope the true scholars will forgive. It will
also be clear that I have had to rely very largely on secondary
sources, though I have checked all the references I can and
have steeped myself in as much of the literature both from
Indian and Western sources as I could lay my hands on or
absorb in the time. Moreover I have quoted from these freely,
with the deliberate intention of putting others on to the trail
of what I have found. I cannot claim in this regard to be
more than one of theology's journeymen. I have felt an obligation in the past to try to fulfil this modest function between
the two sides of the Atlantic and also between the professor
and the pew. But this more recent journey of the spirit has
made me realise how 'one-eyed' the constraints of our West-

ern education and cultural conditioning have made us.

There are three ways (at least) in which I have found that being forced as a Christian from the West to look afresh through Eastern eyes can change and expand one's vision.

The first comes as a corrective to a predominantly one-eyed approach to reality and truth in general. This will be the perspective of the first four chapters, which represent a development of the three Teape Lectures. They will not be concerned with comparing and contrasting Christianity and Hinduism as such: I should feel I needed to have lived with the latter for far longer to make any such judgments. They are concerned rather to plead for a holding together in focus of two 'eyes' on reality which are to be found in both religions, and indeed in all. The line between them cuts right across the different faiths, but in practice one or the other can so dominate a tradition that a distorted perspective arises if the corrective is not present. To be compelled to correct one's vision of reality through study of a tradition in which the other eye dominates is a salutary exercise. For this purpose I have concentrated on the many-faceted religious tradition of Hinduism, since this was where the lectures required me to focus, though in many ways the equally varied Buddhist tradition (or for that matter the Taoist) would have been just as apposite and in some ways more congenial. But my purpose at this point was not to examine either for its own sake or to set it against the Christian tradition as such (or the Jewish or the Muslim), but to allow the way of looking at truth embodied predominantly, but partially, in each to be corrected for distortion.

But, secondly, to plead for a two-eyed vision of reality carries with it a challenge, explicitly to any kind of exclusivism and implicitly to any claim to uniqueness. Though I did not address myself to this in the lectures, I could sense it constantly present beneath the surface of the questions. This comes to a focus in the threat which to others is presented by, and for the believer is presented to, the Christian claim for the uniqueness of Christ. The purpose therefore of my fifth chapter is to reconsider from each side what at this point is being asserted and to ask whether the perspective here adopted can be constructive as well as challenging.

Finally, there is the less threatening, though equally stretching, demand to allow a wider vision not merely to correct but also to complement one's own rather parochial faith – in other words, to make it more catholic. Having been 'there and back again' (to use the title of C. H. Dodd's little-known book of children's stories), one is made to realize how impoverished *on both sides* is the Christianity that has suffered from what a long-term servant and surveyor of the Indian scene has called 'the Latin captivity of the church'. There is so much both in giving and receiving to 'open up' (Matt 2.11), like those first travellers from the East, if we are to worship, or shape the worth of, the Christ. Now that in India the first missionary era of the church is drawing to a close, it would be tragic if indigenization meant isolation. Indeed I count it one of the primary obligations laid on those to whom the lines are still open, whether by the spoken or the written word, to promote that cross-fertilization of which Westcott spoke, perhaps in more florid language than we should dare to use, in promoting the Cambridge Mission to Delhi a hundred years ago:

> By the essential conditions of their life, by the circumstances of their history, by the continuity of their growth through political and religious revolutions, by the catholicity of their sympathy in which they embrace every form of speculation and enquiry, by the happy discipline through which they combine reverence with freedom and enthusiasm with patience, the Universities are providentially fitted to train men who shall interpret the faith of the West to the East, and bring back to us new illustrations of the one infinite and eternal Gospel.

So my final chapter will attempt very modestly – since the real task must be done by Indians and by those who have made India their life – to share something of that continuing task. As I went round the world I was frequently asked, What do you make of liberation theology (from South America) or black theology (from Africa or the States)? No one, even in India, asked me, What do you make of Indian theology? That seemed a pity. For there is a good deal more of it than I certainly realized. But it has not travelled, and only too little of it has been published in the West. If I can do anything here to open up the lines of communication I shall be content.

JOHN A. T. ROBINSON

CHAPTER I

Two Eyes on Reality

Journeying into life

Traditional Hindu teaching has divided the 'ages' of man not, like Shakespeare, into seven but into four. These are the four *ashramas* or stages on life's way. The first is that of the bachelor student, the *brahmachari,* who under the eye of his *guru* or preceptor studies the sacred books in a life of celibacy, frugality and discipline. The second is that of the householder, the *grihastha,* who marries and brings up a family in fidelity to the multifarious duties of his social station. Thirdly comes the stage of the *vanaprastha* or forest-dweller. 'When the householder sees wrinkles (in his face) and whiteness (in his hair) and the son of his son, let him retire to the forest.' Here he withdraws, with or without his wife, to concentrate upon prayer, austerity and religious exercises. Finally there is the *sannyasi* or renouncer, who is free of all attachment to the world and even to the religious round. 'With no friend but the Self' he lives as a wandering mendicant without shelter and without fire, finding his delight only in the quest of inner peace.

This scheme of life is elitist, being at best relevant only to the top three of the four castes, let alone to out-castes, and sexist, having no distinctive provision for women, and is of course inapplicable literally to the circumstances of modern life in India or anywhere else. Yet I start from it as containing a seed of spiritual wisdom not irrelevant to the journey upon which my wife and I found ourselves setting out for the East.

For both of us it was much more than a six-months' safari. It was a voyage of exploration, keeping travelling on, in the hope that, with T. S. Eliot,

> the end of all our exploring
> Will be to arrive where we started
> And to know the place for the first time.[1]

It was the first time we had gone East. 'Go West, young man' has been the call, ever since the Californian gold-rush. And that metaphorically as 'students' we had done time and again, with a new world of knowledge and experience to acquire and absorb. Then as we took on more of the burden of the world came the stage of the 'householder' with commitment to family and responsibility for the concerns and cares of office. As far as these allowed, the call to travel came more from the South and to involvement in the theology of liberation and the struggle for justice. Indeed we began this present journey with a second visit to South Africa, arriving on the day of Steve Biko's funeral and being there for the banning of the Christian Institute. And spiritually one may not leave that world behind while there is yet anything that a white liberal can say or do. But the unexpected invitation to turn East came as a call which secretly I had always funked. This was partly because, in Eliot's words again, 'human kind cannot bear very much reality', and the prospect of treading the pavements of Calcutta among people for whom one was powerless (or unprepared) to do anything was a prospect that one did not naturally seek. But it was also because at a deeper level one would be shaken out of one's presuppositions and compelled to look at truth through a different glass of vision. And this was disturbing if not threatening. Yet it was an invitation that I knew I could not refuse. And fortunately at this third stage of life we were free and able to go together, to explore in the 'forest' of the spirit something of the wisdom of the sage and the seer.

Whether either of us reaches the fourth stage remains uncertain, and speaking for myself I am bound to admit improbable. Yet the goal of the wandering Indian *sannyasi,*

---

[1] 'Little Gidding', *Four Quartets*, p. 59.

as we have been reminded by Swami Abhishiktananda (Dom Henri Le Saux), who was the theme of the previous year's Teape Lectures in Cambridge by Fr James Stuart of Delhi and one of the few from the West literally to have attained it, is in fact remarkably similar in spirit to that of the itinerant messenger of the gospels:

> Like him he is free from all anxiety or preoccupation, being without ties of any kind, whether to things, places or people. Wherever he goes he is a stranger, and yet everywhere he finds himself at home, since he is sovereignly free in his absolute renunciation.[2]

And that in turn is a description which, consciously or unconsciously, echoes the famous account in the second-century *Epistle to Diognetus* (5 and 6) of *all* Christians *in the world,* who live in their own countries as aliens yet bear their share in all things as citizens, for 'every foreign country is a fatherland to them and every fatherland is foreign'. It is a reminder that what value there is in the Hindu *ashramas* is not so much as stages for the few in a pre-urban culture, though the progression still has its validity, but as aspects of a total spirituality for all, if not for each.

The necessity of dialogue

Meanwhile the purpose of these lectures and the exploration they embody was to be open to the third of the four stages – for which the first prerequisite is to sit still and be quiet. Unfortunately the first duty of a visiting lecturer is to go round talking. What he can do, however, is to bring with him his questions, questions that start as they must from where he is, yet in the hope of evoking and listening to the questions that begin from where he is not. In other words, he comes to 'talk across' the space, geographical and spiritual, that separates – that is, in the root sense of that overworked term, for dia-logue. This is to be distinguished from de-bate, which comes from a root meaning to batter down, to defeat. In dialogue it is no part of the purpose to beat the other party,

[2] *Saccidananda,* p. 9.

to oust him from his position. Each respects the centre from which the other is speaking.

But there is an important difference between centres and edges. Each of us, if we are in any way integrated, has a centre from which our lives are lived, and our 'world' is what is enclosed within the circumference of that circle. Yet often we are more *conscious* of the edges than the centres, corresponding to the bounds of an animal's territory which it stakes all to defend. The edges may be hard, the boundaries barricaded, while the centres are relatively unformed. The effect of dialogue is to bring to consciousness, and therefore to strengthen, our centres – so that where we stand will often in the process become clearer and firmer. But we do that by being prepared to soften our edges, to open up the frontiers, and let down our defences.

In dialogue we start from two self-contained circles which may, at most, intersect. The object is not to achieve concentric circles by absorbing one into the other. But neither is it to convince oneself or the other person that the two centres are really indistinguishable. One of the leading exponents of modern Hinduism, Ananda Coomaraswamy, has said that 'the purpose of religious controversy should be, not to "convert" the opponent, but to persuade him that his religion is essentially the same as our own'.[3] But this attitude, which is characteristic of much educated Indian thought, is equally destructive of dialogue. Rather, by retaining the two centres in all their genuine differences, the object is to work towards an ellipse. The centres remain, but the perimeters are broken and pushed out, and in due course begin to join up again to embrace a larger field of experience. This is a process of a life-time, of living and growing and working together, of being stretched, shattered and expanded. But the resulting ellipse, though less cosy to live with than a circle, gains from the polarity, the creative tension, between its two foci.

Consequently the purpose of dialogue is not to eliminate but to respect the differences of centre – for both are essential. Rather it is to articulate and bring them to fuller awareness.

[3] 'On the Pertinence of Philosophy', in *Contemporary Indian Philosophy*, ed. S. Radhakrishnan and J. H. Muirhead, [1]1936, p. 121; [2]1952, p. 159.

In the process of course we may find our centres being questioned and their adequacy being challenged, chipped away or changed out of recognition. We may even be led to abandon them and begin looking at things from another viewpoint. Indeed unless we are prepared for this we should not start: authentic dialogue is dangerous. But in the first instance it is a process of opening up closed frontiers, of letting down defences against access or egress. This can appear to be a threatening experience, yet if we have the courage to be exposed it constantly proves a strengthening and enriching one.

I am only too conscious that real dialogue cannot be conducted from a distance or on a tip-and-run trip. This again is one of the hazards of being a visiting lecturer, especially for the first time, which inevitably means that one's preparation has had to be done 'cold', out of the situation. Klaus Klostermaier in that gem of a book *Hindu and Christian in Vrindaban* has spoken devastatingly of the difference between theology done coolly and collectedly at 70° in the shade and theology at 120°.

> The theologian at 70°F in a good position presumes God to be happy and contented, well-fed and rested, without needs of any kind. The theologian at 120°F tries to imagine a God who is hungry and thirsty, who suffers and is sad, who sheds perspiration and knows despair (p. 40).

Most of my preparation had to be done in a study nearer 50°! Here I can only pay tribute in advance to those who have sweated it out over the years, men like Klostermaier[4] and Bede Griffiths[5], Murray Rogers[6] and Roger Hooker[7] and Ray-

---

[4] See also his essay 'Dialogue – The Work of God' in *Inter-Religious Dialogue*, ed. H. Jai Singh, pp. 118–26; 'Hindu-Christian Dialogue', *Journal of Ecumenical Studies* 5, 1968, pp. 21–44; and *Hindu and Christian in Vrindaban*, especially pp. 101–6.

[5] *Christian Ashram: Essays towards a Hindu-Christian Dialogue; Vedanta and Christian Faith*; and *Return to the Centre*.

[6] 'The Content of a Hindu-Christian Dialogue', *Religion and Society* 6,1959, pp. 68–71; 'Hindu and Christian – A Moment Breaks', in *Inter-Religious Dialogue*, pp. 104–17; 'Dialogue Postponed', *Asia Focus* 5, 1970, pp. 210–19, etc.

[7] *Outside the Camp*, republished as *Uncharted Journey*; 'Three Steps Backwards', *Indian Journal of Theology* (henceforth *IJT*) 24.2, 1975, pp. 1–8; 'Dialogue – Myth and Reality', *New Fire* 3, 1975, pp. 386–9; 'A Disquiet within Hinduism', *New Fire* 4, 1976, pp. 146–9; *Journey into Varanasi*.

mond Panikkar[8], let alone those who have lived and died it
out like Fr Jules Monchanin[9] (1895–1957) and Dom Henri Le
Saux (1910–73), who changed his very name to Abhishiktananda.[10] May they forgive my intrusion.

There is now a considerable literature reflecting upon the
conditions of dialogue,[11] and we should listen to those who
speak out of the experience of such engagement:

> Too often this is set up as an encounter of representatives in a
> contest of comparisons or, worse still, a contest of courtesies. . . .
> But unless it grows out of the gentle delving and slow maturing
> of friendship, dialogue is only an exercise in indifference, the very
> antithesis of love.[12]

> We have to come with complete honesty, ready to hear God
> speaking to us through our partner; ready even to change our
> opinions if God should guide us to do so. And yet we do not
> 'tremble for the ark'; we come trusting in God, knowing that he
> is truth, and that the truth will prevail.[13]

> The only principle of inter-religious dialogue is truth, the only
> way for it to succeed is love. It does not aim at shaking the

[8] Especially *The Unknown Christ of Hinduism* and *The Trinity and the Religious Experience of Man.*

[9] Cf. Abhishiktananda, *Swami Parama Arubi Anandam: Memoir of Jules Monchanin;* J. Mattam, 'Abbé Jules Monchanin and India "the Land of the Trinity" ', in *God's Word among Men,* ed. G. Gispert-Sauch.

[10] See especially 'The Way of Dialogue', in *Inter-Religious Dialogue,* pp. 78–103; *Hindu-Christian Meeting Point; Guru and Disciple; Saccidananda; The Further Shore.*

[11] Apart from the works already referred to, cf. especially: P. D. Devanandan, *Christian Concern in Hinduism* (with a foreword by Radhakrishnan) and *Preparation for Dialogue* (he was the first Director of the Christian Institute for the Study of Religion and Society at Bangalore, which has promoted so much of this in conjunction with the Christian Literature Society of Madras); M. M. Thomas, 'The Significance of the Thought of Paul D. Devanandan for a Theology of Dialogue', in *Inter-Religious Dialogue,* pp. 1–37, together with the remaining essays in that book; J. B. Chethimattam, *Dialogue in Indian Tradition* (from a Roman Catholic viewpoint); R. H. S. Boyd, *An Introduction to Indian Christian Theology,* especially ch. 10; *India and the Latin Captivity of the Church,* especially pp. 116–29; Marcus Braybrooke, *The Undiscovered Christ;* S. J. Samartha, 'Major Issues in the Hindu-Christian Dialogue in India Today', in *Inter-Religious Dialogue,* pp. 145–69, and *The Hindu Response to the Unbound Christ;* J. R. Chandran, 'A Christian Approach to Other Religions', *Bangalore Theological Forum* 7.2, 1975, pp. 1–20; and E. J. Sharpe, *Faith Meets Faith,* pp. 132–49.

[12] John V. Taylor, in the preface to Klostermaier, *Hindu and Christian in Vrindaban,* p. viii.

[13] Boyd, *India and the Latin Captivity,* pp. 120f.

convictions of anybody. Its results must be only to confront more
vividly each of the participants with truth. The sincerity of each
one and his commitment to the Spirit will then act
automatically.[14]

Dialogue involves a readiness to listen to the other *as other*. It
demands a silence in oneself in order to understand the non-
Christian brother as he understands himself.[15]

We are not town-criers of the grace of God, but would be guests
at every man's home for its sake.[16]

Those who have had most experience know most also of
the degree of frustration and failure.[17] Indeed Dom Aelred
Graham at the end of a long life of such encounter has said,
'I see little point in organized dialogue between representatives of the Christian Church on the one hand and Hindu
and Buddhist experts on the other.'[18] Yet no one has been a
better representative than he of what Murray Rogers calls
'the inner dialogue' which is a precondition of the outer and
for which the terms are the same.[19] And it is from this inner
dialogue, if not from the exposure required for the outer, that
this book has been born and to which it forms an invitation.
Immersion in reading and a physical presence, however brief,
is, in this spirit, enough to convict one of how blinkered one
has been.

The thou and the that

But it is time now to pass from form to matter. For the
dialogue I wish to explore is, as I have indicated earlier, not
between two religions as such and their competing truth-
claims. The twin foci are not those of Christianity and Hin-

[14] Abhishiktananda, from an unpublished article 'The Depth Dimension in Dialogue'. I owe the reference to Murray Rogers.
[15] Braybrooke, *The Undiscovered Christ*, p. 73, interpreting Murray Rogers.
[16] Kenneth Cragg in *Study Encounter* 3, 1967, p. 60; quoted in Samartha, *The
Hindu Response*, p. 18.
[17] Cf. especially Rogers, 'Dialogue Postponed' (n.6 above), and Hooker, 'Three
Steps Backwards' (n. 7 above).
[18] 'Can We Learn from Eastern Religions?', *The Ampleforth Journal* 83.2, 1978,
p. 21.
[19] 'Hindu and Christian – A Moment Breaks', in *Inter-Religious Dialogue*,
pp. 111–17.

duism, though my illustrations will be drawn in the circumstances mostly from these two traditions. I am interested
rather in exploring the polarity, the tension, between two
centres which are to be found in different degree within all
our spiritual traditions and indeed within each one of us. This
is in part a dialogue between West and East, but only in the
sense that there are clusters of ideas or presuppositions which
are more dominantly associated with one geographical or
religious tradition than another. Perhaps the nearest analogy
is the dialogue (when it does not harden into debate or sex-
warfare) between male and female. To all appearances each
of us is either male or female: the centres and the edges alike
are seemingly well-defined. Yet modern psychology, as well
as the ancient myth of androgynous man, brings home to us
that we are all both masculine and feminine, just as we are
heterosexual and homosexual, in different proportions.
Indeed we are whole men and women to the extent that we
learn to acknowledge and accept, rather than suppress, the
less dominant factor within us. In the same way, religiously
and culturally we are in W. S. Gilbert's immortal phrase
'elliptical billiard-balls': we are bi-polar, at least.

But to clarify the two centres I have in mind, if they are
not exclusively Hindu or Christian, Eastern or Western, let
me return to the question of how my wife and I came to
arrive in India. It was, as I said, part of a longer journey.
And we came not direct from England, encapsulated in a
pressurized jet, but exposed first to South Africa and all that
that stands for and secondly to Jerusalem and all that that
stands for (and more briefly to the old Islamic centres of
Isfahan and Shiraz). And Jerusalem, as a famous sixteenth-
century map depicts it,[20] stands, spiritually, at the centre of
a clover-leaf joining Europe, Africa and Asia. It has ever been
a place where three ways meet. We approached it from the
south, but it has also been the point where East and West
have come together – and just as vehemently sprung apart.
It is the cradle of faith for us in the West, and the point of
departure from which spiritually we must needs set out to
explore the East.

[20] By Heinrich Bünting in his *Itinerarium Sacrae Scripturae*, Helmstadt 1581.

This, likewise for the first time, was also a necessary part of our personal pilgrimage. For my wife and I have come to where we are today only via a little book written by one who latterly lived and died in Jerusalem. Martin Buber's *I and Thou*, one of the spiritual classics of the twentieth century, was the theme of my PhD thesis and has been the inspiration for many in our generation of what he styled 'dialogical living',[21] or life as dialogue. And it gave definitive expression to one of the poles in the dialogue which I should like to introduce. It is indeed the centre primarily *from* which I have been brought up to speak. It is not specifically Christian – in fact this particular expression of it is Jewish. But it is characteristically Hebraic, in the sense that it is a distinctive and dominant feature of the Jewish-Christian awareness of reality.

For Buber the primary word, prior to all speech, is the double-word 'I-Thou'. In the beginning is relationship. Ultimate reality is not the 'I', whether of the individual or the supreme Being, the ego or the Self. It is the relationship, in the first instance, of I-Thou, though this can fall away into the relation not of subject-subject but of subject-object, of I-It or I-He or I-She. What nothing can do is to fall out of this relationship altogether, and there is one Thou, the eternal Thou, the ground of all relationship who can never become an It. Jesus the Jew gave expression alike to the intimacy and to the ultimacy of this relationship when he spoke of God in terms of '*Abba*', Father, and declared that *nothing* could drop out of this utterly gracious care. It speaks of the irreducibility of the personal and of communion between persons. In the beginning and in the end is relationship, which can never be transcended or absorbed – even in God. There is the closest possible mystical unity between I and Thou, but always it is a mysticism of love, which insists upon and respects the *non-identity* of the other.

This is one centre and, as I said, the dominant centre of the tradition from which I speak. The other centre, the dominant centre of the tradition to which in India I was speaking and from which I have most to learn, is that which insists on

---

[21] *Dialogisches Leben*, Zürich 1947, the title of a composite volume including both *I and Thou* and what was published in English as *Between Man and Man*.

non-duality, advaita. In the place of the primary word 'I-Thou' stands the mystic copula *tat tvam asi*, 'That art thou'.[22] The emphasis is on union rather than communion, on the overcoming of separation and individuation. The norm is nothing less than identity, the return or reabsorption of the ego into the divine or, as Plotinus spoke of it in the Western version of the same tradition, into the One or Illimitable (*to apeiron*). It is the realization that self *is* none other than the ultimate reality, the *atman* is the *Brahman*, the individual soul (*jivatman*) is not separate but one with the Supreme Spirit (*paramatman*). In this state, says Plotinus again, the ecstatic 'has become God, nay, rather he *is* God'. Similarly, within the mainstream of Christian mysticism, Catherine of Genoa exults: 'My "I" is God, and I know no other "I" but this is my God.' Finally the same is to be heard even from within Islam, which more than any other tradition emphasizes the distance between God and man, in the Persian Sufi, Al-Hallaj, who in AD 922 was tortured and crucified for saying 'I am the Truth, or the Real':

> Is there an I *and* a Thou? That would make two gods!
> One Selfhood is there, Thine, for ever
> At the heart of my nothingness.[23]

And Abu Yazid (d. 875) is recorded as saying to Allah, in words strongly reminiscent of the *tat tvam asi*:

> Adorn me in Thy Unity, and clothe me in Thy Selfhood, and

---

[22] *Chandogya Upanishad* 6.8.7–16.3, 'That which is the finest essence – this whole world has that as its soul. That is Reality (*satya*). That is Atman (Soul). That art thou.' Cf. *Brihadaranyaka Up.* 1.4.10, 'Whoever thus knows "I am Brahman!" becomes this All; even the gods have not power to prevent his becoming thus, for he becomes their self (*atman*)'; and *Mandukya Up.* 2, 'For truly, everything here is Brahman; this self (*atman*) is Brahman' (tr. R. E. Hume, *The Thirteen Principal Upanishads*, though amending 'Brahma' to 'Brahman' in accordance with established usage. (Cf. Radhakrishnan, *The Principal Upanishads*.) Panikkar, *The Vedic Experience*, pp. 747–53, interprets the central affirmation *tat tvam asi* to mean that the 'I' of Brahman constitutes the individual self *as a person*, as a 'thou'; '*that art thou*, the thou of the I, the thou of Brahman' (p. 749). But with all deference to his immense knowledge and insight I find it difficult to believe that this suggested interpretation is not a reading of Buber into the Upanishad.

[23] *Muqatta 'at* 35.10.55, quoted Abhishiktananda, *Saccidananda*, p. 61. Cf. Cyprian Rice, *The Persian Sufis*, especially pp. 16f., for the loss or 'noughting' of the self (to use the term of the English mystic, Walter Hilton) in the life and love of God.

raise me up to Thy Oneness, so that when Thy creation see me they will say, We have seen Thee: and Thou wilt be That, and I shall not be there at all.[24]

Perhaps the difference between the two standpoints can best be brought out in some words from an unpublished work of Abhishiktananda on 'the contemplative message of India'.[25] He starts precisely from Buber's position:

> God can never be approached as an object, for an object is always a projection of thought. God is not a He for man to speak about or for thinkers and theologians to discuss. God is a Thou, but . . . a Thou who inhales into himself and as it were annihilates the I which tries to utter, for God is first and foremost an I before whom every I can only be silent.

Buber, on the other hand, with the prophets, would have stressed the God who addresses man and requires of him an answer: 'Son of man, stand upon thy feet and I will speak with thee' (Ezek. 2.1).

In one form or another the absorption or annihilation of the 'I' in the divine Being or ultimate Reality is the *dominant* presupposition of the Hindu and Buddhist traditions, at any rate in their abstract thought, if not in their devotional piety. As I shall be stressing time and again, this does not mean that there is not also much of the other emphasis within them. Indeed a former Teape Lecturer, Ninian Smart, has explored the similar tension *within* the Indian tradition of the 'yogi' and the 'devotee', of *dhyana* and *bhakti*.[26] Yet if Buber the Jew can stand as the representative of one emphasis, then Shankara, the archetypal Hindu philosopher and exegete, can represent the other, the goal of *advaita*. This speaks of the final subordination of the personal to an impersonal absolute, of the inferior *Brahman* (*apara Brahman*) with qualities (*saguna*), who may be addressed as He, to the supreme *Brahman (para Brahman)* without qualities (*nirguna*), who can only be spoken of in terms of It.[27] Multiplicity is subordinated

---

[24] Quoted A. J. Arberry, *Sufism*, p. 55.
[25] 'Le message contemplatif de l'Inde', a reference again supplied to me by Murray Rogers.
[26] In *The Yogi and the Devotee*.
[27] For valuable summaries of this teaching, cf. Swami Nikhilananda, *The Upanishads*, pp. 25–106; Panikkar, *The Vedic Experience*, pp. 652–745.

to identity, everything, in Buddhist terms, to no-thing or the Void (*sunyata*), or in Lao Tzu's phrase to 'the *tao* that cannot be spoken', or the Silence (*sige*) of the Gnostics, or the Abyss (*Ungrund*) of Jacob Boehme. The ultimate reality, beyond all appearances, is the One without a second[28] rather than the One-with-another, the I-Thou.[29] So far from relationship to the other, as in Buber, constituting the indissoluble nexus of all authentic being, 'Where one perceives no other, hears no other, recognizes no other, there', says the Upanishad, 'is fullness'.[30] And even when in this tradition stress is laid, as in Jainism, on the irreducibility of the individual soul, eternal and uncreated, this is conceived in essence as entirely out of relationship. There is no more sense here than in any other Indian system of a personal centre,

> which can enter into close communication with other personal centres *and emerge more of itself.* Where there are no persons, all ties become claims which fetter freedom, and, as a consequence, dreadful austerities must be performed to smash one's way to deliverance. But where there are persons, union in love becomes possible, for love can unite without enslaving; love is not a chain but a link which only heightens freedom.[31]

I have deliberately stated the antithesis in its sharpest form, so as to bring out the polarization. But now I want to stress that the two are not simply exclusive or barren opposites. In fact many in all traditions have held them together in tension, with one playing the dominant, the other the subsidiary role. To most of us each in different degree, or in different mood, makes its appeal – just as in each of us there is the male and female, the *animus* and the *anima*, the *yang* and the *yin*. In fact Friedrich Heiler, who in his classic book on *Prayer* isolated, and in isolation distorted, much the same distinction

---

[28] *Chandogya Up.* 6.2.1.

[29] Buber himself set out the contrast between these two views, though distinguishing carefully between the non-duality in which the soul becomes unified, centred upon itself, and that in which it becomes drowned in divinization. Cf. *I and Thou*, Gregor Smith, pp. 83–95; Kaufmann, pp. 131–43.

[30] *Chandogya Up.* 7.24.1.

[31] L. Pereira, in *Religious Hinduism*, ed. R. De Smet and J. Neuner, p. 200. I can recommend this 'Presentation and Appraisal' by Jesuit scholars of the many aspects of Hinduism, practical and philosophical, as a most valuable survey and source book.

between what he called the 'prophetic' and the 'mystical',
specifically related the former to the masculine and aggressive
element in the psyche, the latter to the feminine and submis-
sive – though almost everything he said about the one was
positive and almost everything about the other negative! For
myself I can only say that unless I felt the attraction (as well
as the repulsion) of both poles I should not be interested in
exploring how they can be held together. The tension is
within, though it is projected and writ large in the two dominant traditions of West and East.

Yet in each, as I have indicated, there are strong elements
of the other present. Thus from within the Christian camp
one could point to Meister Eckhart, as D. T. Suzuki the
Buddhist has,[32] as an almost pure example of unitive mysticism in which God and the soul become completely one. And
Rudolf Otto has done an impressive study of the fundamental
affinity at this point, without minimizing the genuine differences, between Shankara and Eckhart.[33] He quotes Eckhart
for 'God is the same One that I am'[34] and Shankara for 'He
is the Real. He is thy Self. And therefore that art thou.'[35]
Similarly there have been those from the West in recent years,
like Monchanin and Abhishiktananda and Bede Griffiths,
who have found in *advaita* an almost wholly satisfying vehicle
for expressing the heart of the Christian mystery: the unity
whether between Father, Son and Holy Spirit or between
God and the believer can readily be stated in terms of *ekat-
vam*, oneness of essence. In the same vein a contemporary
Indian, Subba Rao, says of Christ in his Telegu lyric:

> Now I know that I am that Eternal Spirit.
> I have become You, and You have become I.
> How then can I worship You?
> How can You worship me?
> Can You and I be torn asunder?[36]

[32] *Mysticism, Christian and Buddhist*, ch. 1.

[33] *Mysticism East and West*. Both work with the distinction Tillich referred to as
the God above or beyond God (*The Courage to Be*, pp. 172–8), Eckhart speaking
of *Deus* and *Deitas*, God and the Godhead, Shankara of *saguna Brahman* and
nirguna Brahman.

[34] Op. cit., p. 12.

[35] Op. cit., p. 98.

[36] *New Songs*, song 1, pp. 4f.; quoted Boyd, *Indian Christian Theology*, p. 277;

For men like these, as for Heiler at the opposite end of the spectrum, the other pole appears to play relatively so minor a part in their experience that it can easily be subsumed. Conversely, within the Eastern traditions, particularly in Hinduism though also in Mahayana Buddhism, strong recognition is given to the place of the personal. Ramanuja with his 'qualified non-dualism' (*vishishtadvaita*)[37] is just as representative as Shankara, and from the *Bhagavadgita* onwards, and especially in the *Bhagavata Purana*, centring on devotion to Krishna, and the Alvar hymns, focusing on Vishnu, and the *Shaiva Siddhanta*, celebrating Shiva, and the poems of Tulsidas, inspired by Rama, the God with attributes, the Lord (*Ishvara*), stands very much in the foreground. *Bhagavan*, the Blessed One, is a more complete revelation of the divine than *Brahman*, the impersonal Absolute. 'The worship of the Impersonal laid no hold upon my heart,' wrote Tulsidas; 'tell me how to worship the Incarnate.'[38] And the love-mysticism of *bhakti* devotion, such as that of the great sixteenth-century contemporaries Vallabha in South India and Chaitanya in Bengal, can show itself every bit as ardent and ecstatic as anything in the Song of Songs or German pietism.[39] And there are similar developments in the gracious figure of the *amida Buddha* in Buddhism or in the dissolving warmth of Sufi devotion at the heart of Islam.

Yet it is not enough to observe that the *boundaries* between the two are far from absolute, and indeed constantly shifting – for, as M. M. Thomas observes, the 'unitive' faiths, as he calls them, are being sucked into the universe of the 'messianic' (and he could have added *vice versa*), so that there is intra-faith as well as inter-faith dialogue.[40] The two *centres* also stand in need of each other if justice is to be done to the polarities of experience. It is the complementarity again in

---

also his quotations earlier from Brahmabandhav Upadhyaya (1861–1907), pp. 69–74.

[37] For a study of this classic figure, cf. J. B. Carman, *The Theology of Ramanuja.*

[38] *Ramacaritamanasa* 7.108; quoted in *Religious Hinduism*, p. 243.

[39] For the great variety and complexity within Hindu spirituality alone, cf. S. N. Dasgupta, *Hindu Mysticism*, especially chs. 5 and 6; G. Parrinder, *Mysticism in the World's Religions*, especially ch. 9.

[40] *Man and the Universe of Faiths*, pp. 45f.

Chinese thought of the *yin* and the *yang*. Or, to take the familiar analogy from modern physics, light cannot, we are told, be exhaustively described in terms either of minute particles or of large waves. What look like two opposite and apparently incompatible explanations are both necessary. Each in isolation gives a false and inadequate picture of reality. And the same has been found to apply, in the realm of what Aristotle called meta-physics, to the ultimate reality of God, for whom after all the symbol of light has been prominent alike in Western and in Eastern religion. Either, it would seem, he must be personal or impersonal, either non-duality or non-identity must have the last word. Yet each set of language in isolation, as we shall see, has led to serious contradictions and distortions and has produced theologies and religious systems which have not only stood towards each other in mutual exclusiveness and negative tension but have succeeded for those outside them, and for many today within them, in rendering God inaccessible and God-talk incredible.

I should like in the chapters that follow to explore such an elliptical model of reality. I have selected two centres, but there could be three or many more. I want to look through two 'eyes' at different aspects of the world in its various dimensions, spiritual and material, and to observe the limitations and distortions that come from our more familiar habit of regarding them from a single centre, and then to see how a second complementary perspective may help to overcome what present themselves as antitheses and contradictions. First, we shall consider the question of God and the personal and how different traditions have fastened on non-duality *or* non-identity, oneness *or* otherness, as the ultimate constitutive reality of life. Then we shall turn to the question of how this ultimate reality is conceived as relating itself or himself to the manifest and the temporal, that is, to the area of the Christ and the historical. Finally, how do these apparently opposite viewpoints regard the world of man and matter and how can their contrary estimates be brought together in a way that is creative rather than destructive?

Obviously over so vast a field no more than hints can be thrown out. But it is the perspective for which I am pleading that matters more than any particular conclusions. As Otto put it in another connection – in speaking of the relation between what he called 'India's religion of grace' (the *bhakti* tradition) and Christianity: 'It is a question of another *darshana*, of another *vision*, of another *eye*. If a change is to come, another eye must first be opened.'[41] And this concept of *darshana* (from the Sanskrit root *drsh*, to see), of intuitive vision or insight, of a way of looking at, or rather into, reality, is an important one in Hindu thought. 'In the religious context it means the sight of a saint or God, therefore also meeting, audience, visit.'[42] It connects with the idea of the 'third eye', the inner eye of contemplative wisdom; and, needless to say, my title *Truth is Two-Eyed* is in no way intended to oppose this – as I found a Hindu in Delhi immediately assumed! But neither is it intended to controvert the gospel reference to the 'single' eye (Matt. 6.22f.; Luke 11.34), where *haplous* evidently means 'sound' or 'clear' (in contrast with 'double' vision), or Jesus's saying that it is better to enter the kingdom of God, or life, 'one-eyed' (*monophthalmos*). This condition may indeed be better than 'having both eyes to be thrown into hell'. But, as the parallel sayings make clear, it is the equivalent to the state of being 'maimed' and 'a cripple' (Mark 9.43–47; Matt. 18.8f.): it is not in itself desirable. Yet by temperament, training or tradition most of us have allowed ourselves to become one-eyed or so monocular in our vision of reality that effectively our 'lazy eye', spiritually speaking, contributes nothing. And some people, not least religious people, deliberately close that other eye, because, in a sense that Jesus did not mean it, it is a cause of 'offence'. They would *rather* be blinkered and bigoted. And if in that mood they pluck it out, it is scarcely likely to save them from hell, and their vision of 'life' will certainly be mean and narrow.

But I am concerned primarily with those of us like myself who have been content almost unawares to look out on reality from the confines of a one-eyed vision. And the habit of a lifetime is not easily undone. We tend to accommodate anything new that comes in – and we pride ourselves on being very

---

[41] *India's Religion of Grace*, p. 110.
[42] Panikkar, *The Vedic Experience*, p. 875.

open – to our existing field of vision, absorbing, for instance, Hindu insights to Christian, as Hindus have long been accomplished at doing, more honestly and explicitly, the other way round. Readiness to look at reality through both eyes at once brings the promise of extra dimensionality and depth, but presents the labour of a fresh learning and focusing process. It also, as we shall see, brings the danger of a mixed or syncretistic vision, which in dealing with Hinduism is again always very present. It is not surprising that many a missionary and theologian has sheered off at this point. But this book is written out of the conviction that neither the labour nor the danger should be allowed to act as a deterrent. For to live in a society of competing one-eyed men represents an impoverished and, in an inescapably unified world, an increasingly dangerous condition.

CHAPTER II

God and the Personal

The personal and the absolute

The primacy of the Thou and the primacy of the That: such in crudest terms is the polarity perennially experienced by those who would give an account of that ultimate reality, the *ens realissimum*, which in his day St Thomas Aquinas said 'all men call God'. We appear to be confronted by an either-or. Surely the truth must finally lie with one side or the other. For any individual one of the two will represent the dominant vision. But each intuition of reality in isolation has been responsible for serious distortions and mutual antagonisms. The 'world' which one man sees cannot be the same as that which the other man sees. Yet each agrees that ultimate reality is one. How do we pass beyond this antinomy?

Let me start, since I am most familiar with them, with the distortions of my own tradition, with what happens when that centre is made self-sufficient.

This tradition, holding to the 'ultimacy' of 'I' and 'Thou', stresses that the categories in which the eternal is to be apprehended cannot be less than those which are required to describe the highest in distinctively personal relationship – the categories of love and trust, freedom, responsibility and purpose. But it is easy from there to jump to the conclusion that God is to be conceived in terms of *a* Person or Super-individual, on the model of a Self which 'has' a world. This is the move that popular theism has made, however much trained theologians may have stated it more carefully. And this notion of God as a Supreme Being envisaged as 'existing', *a se* and *per se*, 'up there' or 'out there', is that against which Paul Tillich pre-eminently among Christian theologians has protested and which led me in my book *Honest to God* to speak of 'the end of theism', albeit with a question-mark.[1] By this I meant not the end or 'death' of *God* (though that was subsequently announced) but of a particular personalistic image of him which even in the West I sensed was having the effect of making him remote and incredible, displacing him from the centre of centres and banishing him to a 'super-world' that comes in, if at all, for most people today only over and above the vital connections of life.

Now one of the interesting by-products of that statement was for me the realization that this theistic image made him as unbelievable for Eastern religious man as it did for Western secular man. A long and perceptive lecture, of which I still have the tape, was given in London, by a Buddhist monk, on 'Buddhism and the Bishop of Woolwich'. I remember too writing a letter to the *Indian Journal of Theology*, one of the very few I gather that journal has ever provoked.[2] There was also a useful popular book at the time by Geoffrey Parrinder, *The Christian Debate: Light from the East*, which lifted the discussion out of the rather phrenetic domestic context. For by pinning the perception of reality as supremely personal to the projection of God as a supernatural Person, a separate personified Being, the effect for both East and West has been to discredit the theistic conviction of the ultimacy of the personal. Even though the *saguna Brahman,* the *Brahman* with attributes, has also been depicted as the cosmic Man, the supreme Person (*purusha*),[3] such a projection has succeeded in making Western theism appear to the sophisticated

---

[1] *Honest to God*, ch. 2.

[2] *IJT* 13, 1964, p. 26: quoted by I. D. L. Clark, 'Twenty-four Years' Journey: A Survey of Vols. 1–24 of *The Indian Journal of Theology*', *IJT* 25, 1976, p. 132.

[3] It begins in the *Rig Veda* (10.90) as the macrocosmic primordial Man, a thousand-footed, thousand-eyed, thousand-headed male figure, who literally comprises the whole of reality viewed under its personal aspect. For its development in the Upanishads, cf. especially *Mandukya Up.* 2.1.1–10; *Katha Up.* 3.11: 4.12f. *Shvetashvatara Up.* 3.7–21; *Brihadaranyaka Up.* 2.3.1–6; 3.9.10–17; also Panikkar, *The Vedic Experience*, pp. 72–7, 729–38; Boyd, *Indian Christian Theology*, pp. 189f., 236f., and Samartha, *The Hindu Response*, pp. 177–180.

representatives of the Hindu and Buddhist renaissances crude and anthropomorphic, 'lower' than the more rarified spiritual and philosophical apperception of the *nirguna Brahman*, the *Brahman* without qualities and therefore without qualifications. Thus Vivekananda, the great apostle of *advaita vedanta* at the end of the last century, wrote in connection with Jesus in a manner reminiscent of the Gnostics:

> To the masses who could not conceive of anything higher than a Personal God, he said, 'Pray to your Father in heaven.' To others who could grasp a higher idea, he said, 'I am the Vine, ye are the branches,' but to his disciples to whom he revealed himself more fully, he proclaimed the highest truth, 'I and my Father are One.'[4]

Similarly Radhakrishnan, his spiritual successor in this century, wrote: 'The worshippers of the Absolute are the highest in rank, second to them are the worshippers of the personal God' – though he admitted that there were several orders lower still, the next being 'worshippers of incarnation like Rama, Krishna, Buddha'.[5]

But from the opposite end of the spectrum let me now state the impression which the isolation of the other centre has left on those whose primary spiritual focus has lain elsewhere. The image, so to speak, of the Hindu view of life – and in some respects still more of the more purist Buddhist negativities – has been of a static monism, in which not merely are dualities overcome but differences are submerged[6] in an acosmic pantheism which denies the values of personal purpose and individual identity. Everything gets absorbed into a nameless, formless *Brahman*, like pollens merged into honey or a river emptying into the ocean or salt dissolved in water, to use the famous images of the Upanishad.[7] All distinctions,

---

[4] *Complete Works* Vol. II, p. 143. Quoted Samartha, *The Hindu Response*, p. 55; cf. pp. 47–61.

[5] *The Hindu View of Life*, p. 32; cf. his *Indian Philosophy* Vol. I, p. 97: 'Personality is a limitation, and yet only a personal God can be worshipped. . . .The moment we reduce the Absolute to an object of worship it becomes something less than the Absolute.'

[6] For the *proper* difference between these two, cf. Panikkar, *The Vedic Experience*, pp. 656–8, 700–4.

[7] *Chandogya Up.* 6.9.1; 6.10.1; 6.13.1f.

individual, moral and religious, dissolve in what seems an undifferentiated Hindu soup.

However unfair an impression, this is often what the West has *seen*, in the same way that the image of God as the great white male upon the throne has been often what the East has seen – and more recently the South, which has liked it even less. Now I do not think these are just caricatures or misunderstandings, which disappear upon further acquaintance. They reflect genuine limitations which can be transcended only out of the dialogue, spiritual and intellectual, which is but now beginning to occur. Hence the importance, for each side, of pushing beyond the contradictions to that coincidence of opposites where alone the highest mystical traditions of both East and West have insisted that God or ultimate reality is truly to be found.

This is not a matter of synthesis in the Hegelian sense, if by that is implied that both thesis and antithesis are stages to be left behind in the onward search. For they are inadequate only in isolation. After all, one cannot 'get beyond' communion with God as 'pure universal love' or the advaitic experience of unqualified union with the Absolute. Rather, it is a question of how one may be true to both of these insights at once, without the exclusive and negative corollaries of a one-eyed approach. Nor is it a matter of syncretism, which has proved the peculiar temptation in religion and particularly in Hindu religion – that is, of taking up partial insights from every quarter, fusing and absorbing them into an all-embracing whole. This is not an attitude to truth and error we should think of adopting, say, in science, with a bit of Darwinianism here and a bit of Lamarckianism there.

That is not to say that we have not much, indeed most, to learn from those who *within their own traditions* have been most open and sensitive to the 'pull' of the other pole. They have not confounded the centres but they have lived with their doors and windows open. Speaking of this kind of spiritual cross-fertilization, John Dunne, the American Roman Catholic, has written:

The holy man of our time, it seems, is not a figure like Gotama or Jesus or Mohammed, a man who could found a world religion, but a figure like Gandhi, a man who passes over by sympathetic understanding from his own religion to other religions and comes back again with new insight to his own. Passing over and coming back, it seems, is the spiritual adventure of our time.[8]

Perhaps I may put the distinctive character of the exercise to which I am urging the reader in this way. What any form of syncretism does is to dissolve the boundaries so as to merge and re-order everything round a single centre, either supposedly a new one, as in the faith of Bahai, or more often by assimilation and subordination to one's own. One imports and absorbs insights which are permitted to complement and enrich, modify and correct, the one-sidedness or parochialism of one's own perception of reality. And this is fine, so long as genuine distinctions are not blurred. But by drawing the insights of another centre into as it were the gravitational field of one's own, so that they come to form part of that 'universe' revolving round its single centre, one is deliberately seeking escape from the tension of living with *both* poles at once. But truth may come from refusing this either-or and accepting that the best working model of reality may be elliptical or bi-polar, or indeed multi-polar.

The panentheistic model

It is coming to seem probable that the least inadequate map of physical reality may in fact be of this kind. There is a fascinating – if sometimes facile – book by a physicist, Fritjof Capra, *The Tao of Physics,* drawing out the correspondences between elementary particle physics and the insights of Eastern religions, especially Taoism.[9] I am not sure that he is right to confine this so exclusively to the *East* – and in conversation he agrees. Alan Watts, one of the pioneer spiritual explorers of our age, in his playful book *Beyond Theology,* says similarly that the modern scientific way of *describing* things and events is much nearer the way in which the mystic

[8] *The Way of all the Earth,* p. vii.
[9] For an interesting earlier attempt, especially in relation to Buddhist thought, cf. L. C. Beckett, *Neti Neti (Not This Not That),* which however was tied to the now discredited theory of continuous creation out of nothing.

feels them. The point they are both seeking to make is that whereas in the everyday 'Newtonian' world of human experience there seem to be relatively secure centres, namely ourselves, from which we measure time and space, and an absolute centre, or sun, of the universe which assures us that 'God's in his heaven: all's right with the world', the deeper we go, both physically and spiritually, the clearer it becomes that such maps will not do. Centres of course there are, but none is absolute. And there are no separate particles or events occupying determinate positions of space or time. What anything *is* depends on the 'system' of which it is a part. Matter consists not of inert building-blocks moved by external forces or of isolated objects bumping into each other like billiard-balls but more of wave-like clusters of probability in a constantly shifting network of multi-dimensional relationships, physical and spiritual. For the reality without is texturally similar to the reality within. Patterns of matter and mind are reflections of each other; the one does not determine the other, as in the old dualistic ways of thinking. Probability is the statistical outcome of the dynamics of the whole system, not the predictable result of a particular cause. The behaviour of things and objects is to be viewed as the behaviour of 'fields' in which everything ultimately interconnects with everything else. Reality is multi-polar, and its unicity comes not from a single fixed point but from its co-inherence at every level. In this 'world', mass is not indestructible but can be and is being constantly transformed into new patterns and particles, racing, dancing, vibrating at fantastic velocities. Its seeming permanence reflects a dynamic balance, not a static equilibrium.

It is not surprising that parallels have been seen here with Buddhist metaphysics, where everything, including the individual self, is in a state of impermanence (*anicca*) and non-substantiality (*anatta*) and of nothing can one say 'it is' or 'it isn't', or with the complementarity of the *yin* and the *yang* in Taoism,[10] or with the Hindu god Shiva in his endless whirl

[10] For its important relevance for theology, cf. two contributions to *What Asian Christians are Thinking: A Theological Source Book*, ed. D. J. Elwood: Jung Young Lee, 'The Yin-Yang Way of Thinking', pp. 59–67, and Khin Maung Din, 'Some Problems and Possibilities for Burmese Christian Theology', pp. 87–104.

of creation and destruction. In Coomaraswamy's words,

> He arises from his rapture, and dancing sends through inert
> matter pulsing waves of awakening sound, and lo! matter also
> dances appearing as glory round about him. Dancing, he sustains
> its manifold phenomena. In the fulness of time, still dancing, he
> destroys all forms and names by fire and gives new rest. *This is
> poetry; but none the less science.*[11]

Spiritually speaking, Watts contrasts what he calls these
'relational and "fieldish" ways of thinking' with 'theological
monarchism'. The trouble, he says, with this Supreme Being
type of theology is not that it is anthropomorphic but that it
is (now) bad anthropomorphism:

> To construct a God in the human image is objectionable only to
> the extent that we have a poor image of ourselves, for example,
> as egos in bags of skin. But as we can begin to visualize man as
> the behaviour of a unified field – immensely complex and com-
> prising the whole universe – there is less and less reason against
> conceiving God in *that* image. To go deeper and deeper into
> oneself is also to go farther and farther out in the universe, until,
> as the physicist well knows, we reach the domain where three-
> dimensional, sensory images are no longer valid.[12]

But one must also say that the opposite model of monistic
pantheism will not do either. For that is based on an absolutist
picture of the universe (as opposed to a multiverse) as unques-
tioning, and now as questionable, as that of monarchical
theism. In his most valuable survey, *The Acknowledged
Christ of the Indian Renaissance*, M. M. Thomas quotes the
perceptive comments of the Indian judge and lay theologian,
Pandippedi Chenchiah, protesting against the religious absol-
utism common to both Eastern and Western versions of this
approach. Reflecting on a consultation in Madras in 1951
with the Barthian theologian Hendrik Kraemer[13], he said:

There is a humorous side to this Barthian-Advaitic, Kraemer-

---

[11] *The Dance of Siva*, p. 78. Italics mine. Cf. also A. R. Peacocke's Bampton
Lectures, *Creation and the World of Science*, Lecture 3, where he also quotes the
same passage, and Appendix A for his response to Capra's book.

[12] *Beyond Theology*, p. 222. Cf. also F. C. Happold, *Religious Faith and Twentieth-Century Man*, who pleads powerfully for the 'intersection' of 'relationship
theology' and 'pattern theology', especially in ch.13.

[13] Best known for his study, *The Christian Message in a Non-Christian World*.

Radhakrishnan duel. Both believe in the Absolute. Both discard relativism, one as sin and the other as *maya*. I am a relativist and don't believe in the absolute, whatever it may mean. . . . Why these blood brothers quarrel I don't know. I consider the absolute a construct of the mind. The absolute is metaphysical while the relative is historic.[14]

Would that all judges were so unmonarchian! Alas, the opposite mind-set seems almost an occupational hazard.

To that final provocative remark about the reality of the 'historic' I shall return in the next chapter. But let me go on now to sketch in broadest outline the kind of understanding of God and the world to which this more 'fieldish' way of thinking would point. This seems to be neither monist nor dualist, nor just a compromise between the two. It has a unicity to it in the sense that everything and every centre of consciousness and energy is interdependent. Yet by the same token it is relational through and through, preserving rather than absorbing differentiation and freedom, multiplicity and movement. God, or *Brahman*, is neither a person outside the process as in theism nor is he identical with it as in pantheism.

Perhaps an analogy may help to illustrate the difference, though like all analogies it must not be pressed. From the point of view of a sub-atomic particle what we call 'the human being' must appear an infinitely complex field of interacting processes exhibiting purely statistical regularities. There is nothing personal about it; everywhere 'chance and necessity'[15] reign. Yet, as *we* know, each of these sub-microscopic 'happenings' is in fact constitutive of an organism expressing an overarching personal purpose. In them all, through them all, 'ultimately' freedom and response and not merely action and reaction are being manifested. This is what makes it distinctively 'human' being. And the *humanum*, requiring for its description and explanation categories of 'spirit' and not simply of 'flesh', to use the biblical distinction, is not just the sum of its constituent parts: spirit transcends flesh and may ultimately be independent of it. Yet equally it is not to be

[14] Quoted, Thomas, op. cit., p. 162. Cf. D. A. Thangasamy, *The Theology of Chenchiah*, especially pp. 86–91; and Boyd, *Indian Christian Theology*, ch. 8, for further study of this interesting figure (1886–1959).
[15] Cf. J. Monod, *Chance and Necessity*.

understood as a centre of consciousness over and above or outside it which 'has' a body. The personality is to be encountered in, with and under what from another point of view is the seemingly impersonal field of relations. In some such way the 'divine' is not a Being beyond or over against creation who 'has' a world. Nor is he just the sum of its parts, a purely naturalistic whole which 'some call evolution, some call God'. There is a distinctiveness, a dimension of transcendence, which demands God-language, just as there is a distinctiveness about fields of particles that constitute human and not merely inorganic or organic being: they are the expression of a purposiveness and freedom which finally transcends and accounts for them.

If one wanted a label for this way of looking at the world, the best one is probably 'panentheism', whose definition is 'the belief that the Being of God includes and penetrates the whole universe, so that every part of it exists in him, but (as against pantheism) that his Being is more than, and is not exhausted by, the universe'.[16] It is the view that God is in everything and everything is in God. There is a co-inherence between God and the universe which overcomes duality without denying diversity. In the mystics in particular there are strong affirmations of identification without identity. At any given focus of time or space they can say: 'This, for me, *is* God and God *is* this.' In Eckhart's words,

> All things become to thee pure God, because in all things thou seest nothing but pure God. Like one who looks long into the sun – what he afterwards may see is seen full of the sun.[17]

Yet it *is* not the sun. Similarly with the 'I' and 'God', there is no simple transference of divine attributes to the subject, no denying the difference, what Kierkegaard called the 'infinite qualitative difference', between the self and its Ground. As the anonymous fourteenth-century author of *The Cloud of Unknowing* put it in another writing, 'He is thy being but

---

[16] *The Oxford Dictionary of the Christian Church*, ad loc. Cf. my *Exploration into God*, US edition, pp. 86–91, British editions, pp. 83–7, on whose argument I have drawn here.
[17] Quoted, Otto, *Mysticism East and West*, p. 211.

thou art not his,'[18] or Krishna as he is represented in the *Bhagavadgita*, 'In Me subsist all beings, I do not subsist in them.'[19] Or again there is the statement from the *Shaiva Siddhanta*, 'He (God) is the life of all that lives and yet not confused with any of them.'[20] What Blake called 'the minute particular' is not swallowed up in an all-embracing whole. Indeed, for the poet or the mystic the very 'thusness' (to use the Buddhist term) of the particular takes on an infinite significance. With Blake again, or indeed the modern physicist, he sees 'a world in a grain of sand'.[21] In the panentheistic vision which forms the climax of the *Gita* (11), Arjuna sees 'the whole (wide) universe in One converged, there in the body of the God of gods, yet divided out in multiplicity'.[22]

Speaking of how the mystic apprehends all things as one with God, Alan Watts says:

> He does not see the reality of God behind the illusion of the creature; he sees God in the very reality, entity and uniqueness of the creature, in its very distinction from God.[23]

As the Russian Orthodox theologian Nicolas Berdyaev recog-

---

[18] *The Epistle of Privy Counsel*, ch. 1.

[19] 9.4; tr. R. C. Zaehner, *The Bhagavad-Gita*, p. 306.

[20] Manikkavacakar, *Tiruvacakam* 22.4; quoted, M. Dhavamony, *Love of God*, p. 349.

[21] 'Auguries of Innocence'.

[22] 11.13; tr. Zaehner. For other panentheistic passages in the *Gita* see e.g. 4.35; 6.30f; 7.7–12; 9.4–9, 15–19; 10.19–42; 13.12–17; 15.12–15. Cf. also *Isha Up.* 1, 'This whole universe is pervaded by the Lord'; *Dhyanbindu Up.* 5, 'As fragance is in the flower, as butter in the milk, as oil in sesamum seeds, as gold in the reef of gold, so God dwells in all objects'; *Katha Up.* 5.17, 'The Inmost Self, in the heart of all creatures abiding for ever.'

From the Sufi tradition I would append a poem from the twentieth-century Persian poet 'Ebrat-e Na'ini, which I transcribed in Isfahan:

> Like light which is not the Sun
> and yet is of the Sun
> So is all this world the Sign
> of God and yet not God.
> We are rays of Truth, not He
> and yet He
> Like light which is of the Sun
> yet not the Sun.
> There! Where you look:
> the point of Revelation.
> Never can you say where He is
> and where He is not.

[23] *Behold the Spirit*, 1947, p. 148; [2]1972, p. 146.

nized, 'Mysticism cannot be expressed either in terms of pantheistic monism or of theistic dualism.'[24] In a truly personal panentheism there is no absorption of the individual into the Absolute. Even in the intensest moments of identification the distinctions of creature and Creator remain. In the closing words of C. G. Jung's *Answer to Job,*

> Even the enlightened person . . . is never more than his own limited self before the One who dwells within him, whose form has no knowable boundaries, who encompasses him on all sides, fathomless as the abyss of the earth and vast as the sky.[25]

I quote that from one who was open to truth from all quarters, not least from Eastern religions, and from a book which is a devastating critique of the limitations of traditional Western theism. Yet this is basically what theism at its best has always sought to represent. Panentheism differs from theism not so much in its content as in its projection, in its way of 'mapping' God as 'the inside' of everything. Following a lead from the mystic way of insight *(anubhava)*[26] or intuition (from the Latin *intus ire*), of the I going ever deeper into itself to find God, we should perhaps, following the hint of an Indian Catholic theologian, better speak of 'inscendence'[27] than of transcendence, in the same way that the English poet and Jesuit Gerard Manley Hopkins found himself having to coin the words 'inscape' and 'instress' to describe the heart of nature. Yet this is after all but a difference of spatial imagery – though which imagery we choose is psychologically important. What panentheism, like theism, is fundamentally concerned to affirm is the 'thouness' of everything, in Hopkins' phrase again, 'deep down things',[28] the gracious heart of

---

[24] *Freedom and the Spirit*, p. 242; cf. his *Spirit and Reality*, pp. 132–7. For a similar attempt within the Indian Christian tradition to steer a mid-course between monism and pluralism, *advaita* and *dvaita*, cf. Mark Sunder Rao, who opted for *ananyatva*, 'non-alterity', in his *Ananyatva: Realization of Christian Non-Duality.* See Boyd, *Indian Christian Theology*, pp. 215f.; Samartha, *The Hindu Response*, pp. 134f.

[25] *Collected Works* XI, p. 470.

[26] For the key position of this category as the chief source of knowledge in *advaita* thought, cf. Samartha, *The Hindu Response*, pp. 152f., and Sister Vandana, 'Reflections of a Christian on the Upanishads', in *Research Seminar on Non-Biblical Scriptures*, ed. D. S. Amalorpavadass, pp. 237–59.

[27] Chethimattam, *Patterns of Indian Thought*, p. 97.

[28] 'God's Grandeur'.

Being. Pantheism, on the other hand, whether in Eastern religion or in Western intellectualism, has traditionally tended towards an aesthetic, impassive, impersonalistic view of life. It makes, as I shall be arguing in the subsequent chapters, for an unhistorical quietism without political cutting edge or involvement with the neighbour; and it plays down evil as partial or illusory. In sum, it depersonalizes and dehistoricizes.[29] Its advantage is that it sees God as the inner truth, depth and centre of all being. And this is a far more promising projection than visualizing God and the world as existences with different centres. Historically theism rejected the depersonalization of God in deism but retained its projection. Can we reject the depersonalization of God in pantheism but retain its projection?

The shadow-side of God

This question, of how we may maintain the conviction of the ultimacy of the personal without personifying on the one hand or depersonalizing on the other, is connected with the other side of the coin, with how we deal with the impersonal and sub-personal in our experience of reality. This is wider than the traditional 'problem of evil'. It includes all those elements in our world or in ourselves which Jung called 'the shadow' – not in themselves evil or sinful, but aspects of reality which we would rather not have to acknowledge or live with, things in the universe that constitute a threat to the personal and which when sensed in ourselves we seek to repress or work off on to others. For experience of life is always ambivalent, at whatever depth we encounter it, within or without. It has many faces, soul-destroying, ugly and evil as well as loving, beautiful and good. And the texture of it is like shot-silk; it strikes as grace, it strikes as terror, and the one face is the obverse of the other. Satan and Christ are both 'sons of God', and Lucifer, the morning star of heaven, is in the biblical

---

[29] Cf. the contrast between what Keshab Chandra Sen (1838–84), leader of the reforming movement within Hinduism, the Brahmo Samaj, called 'Hindu pantheism', and 'Christ's pantheism', quoted in Thomas, *The Acknowledged Christ*, pp. 61,70; and the 'revised pantheism' of his colleague P. C. Mozoomdar, ibid., pp. 83f., 90f.

imagery a symbol for both. In Jewish Hasidic mysticism, Satan is the other side of God: he too, is holy. Equally in Hinduism Shiva is alike creator and destroyer, male and female, with his many limbs dancing within the wheel of fire, terrifying and benevolent, with hands that both cast down and lift up.[30]

Here, if anywhere, wholeness demands a two-eyed approach, yet here again each eye on reality has tended towards a myopic vision, producing distortions in isolation, according to which way of looking, or coping, has been dominant. Again the major traditions of East and West have not been exclusively identified with either one or the other, yet the more active Western prophetic approach has characteristically been dominated by one response, the more passive Eastern mystical approach by another.

Faced with the shadow, the unacceptable, the former's response has been to reject and exclude it. The dark has been detached from the image of God or the Christ and projected on to a Devil or Antichrist viewed as the embodiment of evil *per se* – though at the beginning of the process, as in the book of Job, it was not so: Satan was among the agents of God and seen as doing his work, the hand of the Almighty, albeit his left hand. And like God in this tradition he is personified, an *alter ego*, whether (since evil is always divisive) as a 'legion' of demonic spirits or as gathering into a single supreme head everything that God is not. This process comes to its climax in Zoroastrianism, post-exilic Judaism, Islam, and not least in Christianity, where the Devil came to occupy a uniquely powerful, even obsessive, position. The absolutizing of evil in a totally malignant Being has been the dark side of the absolutizing of the good in ethical monotheism. Evil is utterly banished and excluded from God. As Charles Davis puts it, 'God refuses his shadow side and identifies himself with unalloyed goodness, the Devil emerges as God's unconsciously produced shadow. . . . The mystery of iniquity is placed alongside the mystery of goodness.'[31]

The relationship between the two is one of polarization and

---

[30] For a popular account cf. Zaehner, *Hinduism*, pp. 84–7.
[31] *Body as Spirit*, pp. 116f. and ch. 5 *passim*. Cf. Watts, *The Two Hands of God*.

antagonism. Characteristic phrases from this tradition are 'Get thee behind me, Satan' and 'Depart from me, ye that work iniquity'. The demons are silenced and cast out, as the scapegoat is driven off into the wilderness to bear away the sins of the people. Satan is hurled from heaven, trampled under foot, locked in the abyss, thrown into the lake of fire. In Gnosticism too, as Jung points out,[32] the Christ is viewed as 'casting off the shadow' with which he was born, and this for the Gnostic world-view includes all 'the works of the female', a recurrent feature of the shadow-side of the God created in the image of male domination. In order to become acceptable, 'the female must become as the male'. As the final saying of the *Gospel of Thomas* puts it, 'Every woman who makes herself a male will enter the kingdom of heaven' (114).

In this tradition God and the Christ are associated only with the good half: 'Throw away the worser part', says Hamlet to his mother.[33] But splitting the image in this way can give rise to every kind of disintegration and distortion, as Davis again draws out:

> If we take the polarity of good and evil as we find them in human existence, and then identify God the Absolute with a goodness excluding evil, we make it impossible for us to accept ourselves radically. . . . The Devil represents all that we will not acknowledge in ourselves.[34]

When evil is disowned it becomes monstrous and sadistic: 'Demonography is in fact a scarcely concealed pornography.' Worse, it becomes projected on to other people – witches, Jews, blacks. Unacknowledged, it becomes terrifyingly inhuman. And by this polarization not only does the Devil become remote and alienated – 'out there' or 'down there' – but God himself 'formed in the image of a self-righteous monarch, cut off from all the pain and suffering, the frailty and sin of this world, personified moral goodness made absolute,'[35] becomes a very devil, Blake's Nobodaddy, rather than the God and Father of our Lord Jesus Christ. Furthermore, by splitting the Christ-image, by disowning the shadow and identifying

---

[32] *Aion.* Collected Works XI. 2, pp. 41f.
[33] *Hamlet,* Act III, Sc. 4, line 156.
[34] *Body as Spirit,* pp. 117f.
[35] Ibid., p. 124.

it with one half of the personality, it is, as Jung insisted, weakened rather than strengthened. The effect is to make the Christ unreal as a man. He becomes an immaculate paragon, unsullied by any contact with evil, rather than a genuine man of flesh and blood who is 'made perfect', as the Author to the Hebrews boldly puts it, who achieves integration in the only way men can grow, by acceptance and incorporation of the whole self rather than by rejection or repression of a part. For only thus can he '*become* a merciful and faithful high priest' (Heb. 2.17), only so could he save or salve others and communicate to them *his* 'peace', his fullness.[36]

So much for the first of the two one-eyed approaches. The other proceeds from the opposite premise, not of rejection and repulsion but of acceptance and resignation. And this has much to commend it as a starting-point. 'I accept the universe,' said the lady. 'Gad! she'd better!', replied Carlyle. And to accept the universe is to accept the fact that for most people most of the time it is predominantly depersonalizing and depressing. 'All is suffering (*duhkha*)' is the First Noble Truth propounded by the Buddha. Decay and finally death are the inescapable realities to be faced by all. And since they are not to be denied, they must be lived with. Resignation is the key to the only victory of the spirit to be won through them or over them. Moreover all the elements in experience, good and evil, are given together as complementary and opposite poles of the same round of temporal existence, or *samsara*. Everything we are and do is mixed with a great deal of dirt, and the lotus grows only out of the mud. So in the polyphony of life there are gods many and lords many, *devas* who, though divine beings, are themselves caught up in the wheel of existence, elemental powers both creative and destructive. And the polarity of the universe is nowhere better reflected than in the two deities of Hinduism, Krishna and Kali, both in their different ways associates of the all-embracing, all-consuming Shiva.[37]

---

[36] I have here summarized some sentences from my book *The Human Face of God*, pp. 87f., where I go on to relate this to the understanding of the sinlessness of Christ (pp. 88–98).

[37] I am not suggesting that this is *the* response of Hinduism to the problem of evil. Indeed it has no single answer: '*All* the possible solutions are there, somewhere,

In a percipient study, *The Sword and the Flute*, David R. Kinsley has analysed the aspects and antinomies for which they stand and how they are united and related. Of Krishna he says:

> He is the embodiment of all that is implied in the word *lila* [play]: light, almost aerial activity, boisterous revelry, frivolity, spontaneity, and freedom . . . Here God plays, posing himself in ecstatic, spontaneous revelry. Here life is celebration, not a duty. Here life does not grind along but scampers in dance and rejoices in song. All that makes life in the pragmatic world endurable is to be found here. This is the other world of the divine, from which beauty, freedom, and bounty proceed. Here the bondage of necessity does not exist.[38]

By contrast the mere description of Kali, the dark mother, is sufficient to chill the blood:

> Of terrible face and fearful aspect is Kali the awful. Four-armed, garlanded with skulls, with disheveled hair, she holds a freshly cut human head and a bloodied scimitar in her left hands and makes the signs of fearlessness-assurance and bestowing boons with her right hands. Her neck adorned with a garland of severed human heads dripping blood, her earrings two dangling severed heads, her girdle a string of severed human hands, she is dark and naked. Terrible, fanglike teeth, full, prominent breasts, a smile on her lips glistening with blood, she is Kali whose laugh is terrifying. Her flowing, disheveled hair streaming over her left side, her three eyes as red and glaring as the rising sun, she lives in the cremation ground, surrounded by screaming jackals. She stands on Shiva, who lies corpselike beneath her.[39]

Here the repulsive – though not, it must be stressed, the *morally* evil – is taken into the deity with a vengeance. Kali was to become the material of passionate – and tender –

---

so that Hinduism itself offers the full spectrum of varieties of religious experience, the diversity essential to a complete theodicy', Wendy D. O'Flaherty, *The Origins of Evil in Hindu Mythology*, p. 376. Despite the disarming disclaimer, 'This book tells more about Hindu theodicy than most people will want to know' (p. 376), she says in fact very little about Kali and evidently was not in a position to take into account Kinsley's book mentioned below, which was published by the same press the previous year.

[38] *The Sword and the Flute*, p. 78.

[39] Ibid., p. 1, quoting a traditional account. For further gruesome details of her mien, cf. the description on p. 81.

devotion for two of the greatest figures of Bengali spirituality, Ramprasad in the eighteenth century and Ramakrishna in the nineteenth. Through them she is still the object of an intensely popular cultus centred on the Kalighat in Calcutta. As the black goats are beheaded and the funeral pyres blaze, the Black Goddess is served and placated:

> But alongside many of her images . . . , Ramakrishna and his wife are shown sitting placidly. Kali stands behind them, looking terrible as ever, but her hands are placed gently on their heads. There she stands, lolling tongue, bloodied sword, and all – but comforting her trusting children. She is tamed.[40]

By 'taming' (if this is indeed the proper word) those ineluctable aspects of experience for which Kali stands, the dominance of existence by *maya* (delusion), *prakriti* (nature), *duhkha* (suffering) and *kala* (time), all that makes life 'solitary, poor, nasty, brutish and short', is overcome and absorbed by a sort of catharsis, a purging of pity and terror that brings *moksha*, release.

Whether through Krishna or Kali the devotee seeks escape, like the frenzied Maenads in the *Bacchae*, from the iron regimen of *karma* and the remorseless regularities of inauthentic existence. Death as much as love is embraced as a boon, because only by full and bloody acceptance are its terrors drawn and the spirit set free to dance and shout. *Eros* and *thanatos* rejoice together in the *danse macabre* that signals the transcendence of human bondage and in particular of 'the ordered, artificial routine of citified and civilized man'.[41]

I have tried to enter as sympathetically as I can into something which even Rabindranath Tagore as a Bengali found repellent. But whether through the way of the maenad or of the mystic the presupposition of this approach is union with the Absolute beyond the screen of appearances, of suffering and time, good and evil, and the gods themselves. Salvation with the Buddha too is rising above Mara, the Evil One, the *devas* and the whole round of *samsara*.[42] There is the promise

---

[40] Ibid., p. 124.
[41] Ibid. p. 158.
[42] Cf. T. O. Ling, *Buddhism and the Mythology of Evil*, especially ch. 5, on the comparison of Mara and Satan.

of rising above it – but again not of integration. The pain of existence, the dark side of life, is accepted rather than rejected, yet only so as to attain to the still point where it cannot touch or disturb. Similarly the Gnostic ideal is to pass beyond good and evil, to achieve a state of immunity of the spirit to the things of earth.

Each of the two eyes on reality has its strength. Yet each in isolation produces again a distorted and inadequate view of the world. In both there is victory for the personal, the spiritual, but at the expense of failing to incorporate and transform the accusatory (the literal meaning of 'diabolic') elements in experience, the whole surd-like substratum of life as *prakriti* and *samsara*. The unity of reality at the ultimate level is threatened by the failure to integrate the shadow. The Devil is vanquished not by love but by love's denial, destruction and death. Even Shiva, Kali's spouse or 'other half', does not integrate her but is dominated by her sexually and lies beneath her feet: 'He subdues her, certainly, but only by humiliating himself.'[43] Equally Krishna as amorous dalliance and paradisal bliss has no power or mind to integrate the shadow. 'His entire life . . . "accomplishes" nothing'[44] – and is not meant to: it is witness to the divine as purposeless play, as the sheer superfluity of cosmic delight. For the world, as Shankara said, and all that is in it is related to God as motiveless creation, like breathing in and breathing out.[45]

By contrast the great strength of the panentheistic position is that it makes God the personal, yes, the loving, ground of *all* being, of the impersonal and evil as well as of the moral, of volcanoes and tape-worms and cancer as much as of everything else. This is *not* to say that God is morally evil but that his is the ultimate responsibility, through all the random movements of chance and necessity, for everything that happens. He is not the author of what German distinguishes as *das Böse*, wickedness; but he is still the source of *das Übel*, evil in the sense of that which denies and frustrates the fulfilment of personal being.

[43] *The Sword and the Flute*, p. 108.
[44] Ibid., p. 77; cf. pp. 73–8.
[45] *Brahma Sutra*, ed. Radhakrishnan, p. 362.

For all its stress on the moral goodness of God, this recognition is not burked in the prophetic tradition: 'Shall there be evil in a city, and the Lord hath not done it?' (Amos 3.6); 'Out of the mouth of the Most High proceedeth not evil and good?' (Lam. 3.38); 'What? Shall we receive good at the hand of God, and shall we not receive evil?' (Job 2.10). This is above all the corollary of the boundless vision of God, before whom the nations are but a drop in the bucket, of that unknown prophet of the exile, Deutero-Isaiah: 'I form the light, and create darkness: I the Lord do all these things' (Isa. 45.7). I have deliberately in citing these texts retained the Authorized or King James Version because modern versions in their proper desire not to attribute malevolence to God tend to soften the translation to 'calamity' or 'woe'. But the full force of the meaning comes out in another passage from the same prophet in the blunt version of the *Good News Bible*: 'I create the blacksmith, who builds a fire and forges weapons. I also create the soldier who uses the weapons to kill' (Isa. 54.16). God has indeed many faces and hands, like Shiva, whose *shakti*, or energizing power, streams forth in the dance of life.

If, passing beyond the Old Testament, the Christian goes on to say that in the human face of God, in Christ and him crucified, he sees the clue to the rest, it is because it not only accepts but transfigures all the rest: 'at the last through wood and nails'.[46] Meditating on the cross (with its extremes of devotion to the sacred heart and the precious blood) is in some ways the equivalent of meditating on Kali. It is looking in the face, accepting into oneself, the worst that evil and the forces of inhumanity can do. It is being ready with St Paul to be 'crucified with Christ' (Gal. 2.20), just as Kali invites her devotee 'to make of *himself* a cremation ground so that she may dance there.'[47] But the difference is that what the Christian sees on Calvary is the mind and heart of *love*, and its victory is one of resurrection, of incorporation, and not simply of release 'beyond this whirligig of *samsara*'. And the

---

[46] For a profound reflection on this theme out of the agony of experience and failure, cf. Una Kroll, *Lament for a Lost Enemy*.

[47] *The Sword and the Flute*, p. 159.

love is not an *eros*, whether conceived as the dark passion of
Kali or the lithe ecstasy of Krishna, but an *agape* which
absorbs and transforms the sub-personal and barbaric.

In the panentheistic vision, God is no more outside evil
than anything else – nor is he beyond good and evil. As Jung
daringly suggested in proposing to substitute a quaternity for
a trinity,[48] evil is somehow in God. Yet again he is *not* evil in
the only sense which Kant saw was ultimately evil, that of
the evil will. He is love; but a love which all along is taking
up, changing, Christifying everything. In the mass of nature
and history, both without and within, the reduction of all
things to the purposes of spirit, the vanquishing of 'vanity'
by love, seems utterly remote. Over most of the processes of
what Teilhard de Chardin called this 'personalizing' universe
it is still waste and void and darkness. The reason why the
Christian sees hope *in* the process and not *simply* beyond it
is that he claims that a light has shone from within the
darkness, in the face of Jesus as the Christ, which even the
darkness cannot quench. And that is because *his anubhava*,
or insight into reality, grounded in the Bible, speaks of a God
who is not enmeshed in the endless cycle of nature and history, but *is* 'accomplishing' something, who himself has not
done till he is all in all *as love* (I Cor. 15.28).

The diaphany of the divine

That takes us directly into the theme of our next chapter, the
Christ and the historical. But in closing this and to bring it
from the world of theological 'isms' to the life of 'meeting'
from which Buber started I would earth it again in a novel
from which I quoted in my *Exploration into God*, as still the
best exemplification I know of the meaning of panentheism
in the real world of flesh and blood. I refer to *Incognito*, by
the Romanian ex-communist Petru Dumitriu. It also has a
characteristically 'two-eyed' vision, combining the insights of
East and West, not this time on the world scale but in Europe,
steeped as it is both in the spirituality of Eastern Orthodox

[48] See especially his *Answer to Job*, Collected Works XI, pp. 355–470.

religion and in the secularity of the Marxist revolution. It
speaks of the God dwelling incognito at the heart of all things,
disclosing himself in and through and despite the corruptions
and inhumanities of life in our generation. Its theology is
unashamedly panentheistic, though it never uses the term.
God is in everything and everything is in God, literally everything, personal and impersonal, material and spiritual, evil
as well as good. Yet nothing could be further from the typical
world of pantheism, in which the individual loses his significance in an impassive quietism, without any real involvement
in the depths of suffering and sin or in the struggle for freedom
and justice. Here we are in an intensely personalistic, highly
politicized world, in which everything depends upon the
utterly individual response of love. Indeed it is this that gives
the world its meaning and makes it possible to speak in terms
of 'God' at all and to address the whole of life, however,
dehumanizing, with the creative transforming word of 'Thou'.

I could convey the real flavour of that novel only by quoting
more from it than there is space for here.[49] But it expresses
what Teilhard de Chardin called 'the diaphany' of the divine
shining forth (though often through a glass darkly) 'from the
depths of every event, every element'.[50] In the same mood the
Isha Upanishad (6) says, if indeed this *is* here the meaning:
'He who sees the *atman* (the Self) in all things and all things
in the *atman* does not shrink away from or refuse anything'.[51]
All things are in God and God is in all. Even in the vilest
degradation and inhumanity Dumitriu speaks of 'that dense
and secret undergrowth which is wholly composed of personal
events'. This is the network of what Teilhard called the *milieu
divin*, the divine field. From wherever we happen to be, we

[49] See more extensively my review-article 'God Dwelling Incognito', in *But That
I Can't Believe!*, pp. 64–70, and *Exploration into God*, US edition pp. 91–6, British
editions pp. 87–92. Davis cites some of the same excerpts as the climax of his chapter
'The Inhumanity of Evil', *Body as Spirit*, p. 123.
[50] *Hymn of the Universe*, p. 28.
[51] Aurobindo, *The Upanishads*, p. 65, agrees that this is the sense. Hume, *Thirteen Upanishads*, p. 363, translates 'does not shrink away from Him', i.e. the Self,
with a note: 'The indefinite word *tatas* may mean "from these beings", or "from
this Self" or "from this time on", or pregnantly all these.' Zaehner, *Hindu Scriptures*,
p. 165, takes it to refer to the Self; Panikkar, *The Vedic Experience*, p. 811, simply
says 'is free from fear' and Nikhilananda, *Upanishads*, p. 206, 'does not hate anyone'.

shall see it like shot-silk, sometimes in personal categories, sometimes in more impersonal. For many are the faces of God and of the universe, combining numerous apparent contraries.

The two centres from which I began are but two poles in an interrelated mass. From whichever one we naturally start, whether from the I-Thou or the *tat tvam asi*, we must maintain the tension with the other. They are not saying the same thing (and to claim that 'ultimately' they are or that all religions lead to the same point does not help). Moreover in isolation or in fusion they lose their charge. The aim is not syncretism or absorption, but more like what has been called a 'unitive pluralism'.[52] And for this purpose, dialogue, whether inner or outer, is vital. In such dialogue each of us, or each part of us, whether by temperament or tradition, will inevitably tend to represent one or the other viewpoint more powerfully. We all of us have a stronger eye, which will control how we see things. We are bound, as Shakespeare said, to 'speak what we feel'.[53] Or as Jung put it, reflecting on his visit to India, each of us has his own truth to make:

> I studiously avoided all so-called 'holy men'. I did so because I had to make do with my own truth, not accept from others what I could not attain on my own. I would have felt it as a theft had I attempted to learn from the holy men and to accept their truth for myself. . . . I . . . must shape my life out of myself – out of what my inner being tells me, or what nature brings to me.[54]

For myself I shall want to stress what I have called 'the ultimacy of the personal'.[55] And in the chapters that follow on further aspects of this same divide I shall be pressing the claims, as I see them, for the values of the historical and the material. We must speak from where we are, looking out on the world from our vision of it, demeaning neither our centre nor that of the other person. But always it will be for the sake of that creative tension-within-unity which, I am convinced,

[52] R. E. Whitson, *The Coming Convergence of World Religions*, especially pp. 35–53, 166–87.
[53] *King Lear*, Act V, Sc. 3, line 326.
[54] *Memories, Dreams, Reflections*, p. 257.
[55] See the autobiographical prologue to *Exploration into God*, 'Quest for the Personal'.

CHAPTER III

The Christ and the Historical

Two valuations of history

In the opening chapter I spoke of two centres, two poles, from which historically and culturally we have been brought up to look at truth and reality. They are not, I insisted, by any means simply to be identified with the differences of approach of West and East, Christianity and Hinduism. The two are to be found in each camp – indeed the polarity exists to some degree in every individual, and wholeness depends on preserving the tension between both rather than on one absorbing or excluding the other. Nevertheless, in each tradition there is a dominant strain. The one, with its concern for the ultimacy of the relationship, and therefore of the distinction, between I and Thou, is specially characteristic of the Hebraeo-Christian tradition. The other, with its goal of non-duality, of *tat tvam asi* and *nirvana*, is equally characteristic of the Hindu-Buddhist outlook. Then we looked at these two approaches from the point of view of their understandings of God and the personal, both on their positive and on their 'shadow' side, and I urged against the one-sidedness alike of traditional theism and of traditional pantheism the claims of a panentheistic understanding of truth and reality which can overcome the limitations and distortions of each in isolation. Now I want to examine that same polarity under the aspect of 'the Christ and the Historical'.

Before proceeding further I would draw attention to the wording '*the* Christ and the historical', not just 'Christ and the historical'. From very early days in Christianity – and the process is virtually complete even in the writings of St Paul – Christ became a proper name for Jesus, even though it signified more of him than simply the historical figure from Nazareth, in much the same way that the Buddha came for all practical purposes to be identified with the historical figure of Siddhartha Gautama. Yet each of course is a title, 'the anointed one', 'the enlightened or awakened one', and I want to preserve the titular use, as in practically every case does the Gospel of John, because 'the Christ' is wider than Christianity. It is of course in the first instance Jewish. But *Christos*, the Christ figure, can stand also for the broader notion of the 'visibility of the invisible',[1] the mystery of *theos*, of the ultimate reality of God, or *Brahman*, made manifest, embodied in history. It is what the Greeks called the *Logos*, which is consubstantial with both God and man; it is the *avatara* or 'descent' of God in human form, or, in Jungian terms, the God-image in us, the archetype of the self. 'The Christ' in this sense covers a concern as wide as humanity, though the actual word may appear to exclude the Hindu and the Muslim, just as the actual word 'God' may appear to exclude the Buddhist. But in what I shall be saying my primary purpose is to address myself to the significance of the historical, and of involvement in the historical process, *whether or not* that is focused in an incarnation which is regarded as in some way unique. To the implications of the latter claim I shall return in chapter 5.

So let us begin by looking again at the two perspectives on truth represented on the one hand by the Hebraic and on the other by the Vedantic, by what Heiler contrasted as the prophetic and the mystical (though there are some streams of mysticism, such as that of Hasidic Judaism in which Buber stood, which would recognize no such antithesis).

The former is characterized by a strong emphasis on the God of history in contrast both with the *baalim*, the gods of nature, and with the still-life deity of the philosophers whom Pascal was to set against 'the God of Abraham, Isaac and

[1] A phrase Panikkar takes over from Irenaeus in *The Trinity and the Religious Experience of Man*, p. 49.

Jacob'. Even creation is seen as the opening act of history: it represents not an emanation or self-differentiation of the divine as in Eastern religions but the beginning of his works, the expression of his will. For this tradition God is to be known for what he is in his acts, in his purposes for history. 'I will be what I will be' or 'I become what I become'[2] is a less misleading translation of his 'name' than 'I am what I am' (Exod. 3.1–15). The test of his lordship is what shall come to pass. Ultimate reality is that which will finally be realized. The distinctive Hebraic virtue is hope, which is often hardly to be distinguished from faith or faithfulness. God is to be met primarily on the frontiers of social change; he is to be responded to in the *kairos*, the moment of decision. Time and the redemption of time, the fullness of time and the end-time, are alike the medium and the message. History is purpose-ful, it moves towards a goal: it has a direction like an arrow shot at a mark, it does not just go round in circles. And yet it focuses not simply on some consummation at or beyond the close of history; it expects a Messiah, a decisive inbreaking into history. And this in the New Testament is declared to have happened in the midst of history, in the fullness of time.

So Christianity is a historical religion in a further sense. It is not simply that like Judaism it has a high view of the temporal process as the locus of the divine. It is that it sees the clue to the process not just in a final winding-up of which by definition there can be no record, but at a point in time attested by documents *which themselves claim that the veracity of the history is integral to the meaning of their message.* For the early church wrote not simply epistles or spiritual discourses, psalms or manuals of discipline, commentaries or apocalypses (like the contemporary Qumran community by the shores of the Dead Sea), but gospels, a unique literary form which linked its proclamation to certain historical events and a certain historical person. And if these events had never

[2] See Jung Young Lee, 'Can God be Change Itself?', *Journal of Ecumenical Studies* 10, 1973, pp. 752–70, for a most suggestive reinterpretation in terms of the metaphysics of the Chinese Book of Changes, the *I Ching*, of God as the 'all-changing changeless', the still centre of the whirling wheel. Cf. also Barry Wood, *The Magnificent Frolic*, for re-envisaging God, according to the thought-forms of the Hopi American Indians, in terms of be-ing rather than being.

happened or the person had been quite different, the apostles of that message would on their own confession have been found liars. Moreover they claimed that in some sense (and in what sense we must return to) these events had a uniqueness and finality which gave them a significance different from all other historical events. They tied eternal salvation to a moment of time, which ever since, particularly outside a tradition which could conceive anything decisive happening in history anyhow, has proved what has been called a 'scandal of particularity'. And the offensiveness has been increased by the fact that the central scene in this drama has been of a Christ crucified between two criminals and raised to life on the third day. This has been, as St Paul already recognized, not only a stumbling-block to the Jews, and later to Muslims, who shared the same historical matrix, but foolishness to the Greeks, and subsequently to Hindus and Buddhists, who did not.

For the other centre, the other pole, has in contrast been one where history, and still more historicity, has been accorded little significance. It has worked with what has appeared to be an almost opposite estimate of the time-process. Its symbol has been the wheel rather than the road.[3] History as such, in contrast with nature on the one hand and spirit on the other, has been seen to have no distinctive or independent valuation. In the West this was notably true of Gnosticism, of the mystery religions, and of many aspects of Greek thought. Even though the Greeks (unlike the Sanskrit authors) also produced the fathers of modern history-writing, history as such never seems to have found a place either in their metaphysic or in their mythology. For the Platonic tradition time was simply the moving image of eternity, and for the Aristotelian the Absolute was totally timeless and static. Of the East (though qualifications would certainly need to be made of China) the Indian Christian, M. M. Thomas has written,

> It remains largely true that the religious culture of India never came to distinguish radically between nature and history.

[3] Cf. Newbigin, *The Finality of Christ*, pp. 65f.

Indeed one may interject that while the term *prakriti* more or less corresponds to 'nature', no distinctive word for 'history' ever appears in Sanskrit glossaries. But let me continue the quotation:

> Nature is the realm of necessity and knows no freedom to make history possible. And Hinduism, popular Hinduism at any rate, accepted the cycle of nature as the pattern of man and the cosmos. Higher Hinduism with its emphasis on mysticism made self-realisation totally spiritual, with no relation to nature, so that the tension between spirit and nature never became the essence of human selfhood; and without that tension the idea of finite freedom cannot have substance, and spirituality becomes a-historical; so that both Hindu naturalism and Hindu mysticism ran parallel to each other and unable to make men aware of life as historical destiny.[4]

To this way of thinking salvation is not the redemption of time so much as redemption from time, release from the wheel of existence. Both Hinduism and Buddhism have offered liberation (*moksha*) as escape from, a rising above, the round of *samsara* and *maya*, the latter being not so much illusion as such but a delusory way of viewing reality, taking the shadow for the substance. For there is no ultimacy here, no decisiveness, no purpose and no consummation.

> India gives no genuine *worth* to the world because it knows nothing of a *goal* to the world. . . . It is always at the end consumed by fire. But it is never 'transfigured'.[5]

It is not necessarily meaningless or depressing: it is play (*lila*), whose overtones are of joy not jest. Creation is cosmic delight, arising afresh in endless repetition, and the dance goes on till time's great cycle starts again. Whether in the 'still' visions of reality beyond the flux of becoming so characteristic of the Vedantic, Jainite and Buddhist spiritualities or in the passionate tumultuous whirl of Krishna, 'the divine', says Kinsley, 'does not express itself in any essential way through history'. Speaking of Krishna's sojourn at Vrindavan, he observes that it serves no 'purpose':

---

[4] *The Christian Response to the Asian Revolution*, pp. 70f.
[5] Otto, *India's Religion of Grace*, pp. 73f.

He simply overflows himself. He does not reveal himself so much
as he displays himself. He does not act decisively in a historical,
moral, or cosmic sense. He simply lifts the curtain, as it were, on
his inmost being, which is revealed to be self-delight. He reveals
the Godhead to be unconcerned with and aloof from the world,
totally immersed in its own dazzling beauty.[6]

It is noticeable that, even when in modern Hindu writers
like Vivekananda[7] and still more Aurobindo this outlook is
combined with an evolutionary perspective, evolution (*pari-
nama*) remains the unwinding of a previous involution (*pra-
laya*). 'We are bound . . . to suppose,' wrote Aurobindo, 'that
all that evolves already existed involved.'[8] There is nothing
genuinely new, no radical creativity, simply the spinning of
an ever more complex and rarified web out of the body of
nature, which from another point of view is *Brahman* seeking
self-manifestation. And when the process is finished it starts
all over again. We are more in the world of Hegel's philosophy
of spirit than in that of Darwin or Marx. Or rather, as one
of Aurobindo's admirers and interpreters has said of his mas-
terpiece, 'Perhaps the closest parallel to . . . *The Life Divine*
is the *Enneads* of Plotinus.'[9] And that is a world where history
is entirely swallowed up in mystery.

When we come to 'the Christ' in this tradition, in the
broadest sense of that which mediates the changeless reality
of *Brahman* to the world of flesh and blood, there is again a
very different attitude to historicity. The *avatara* is essentially
a divine theophany, God taking human or indeed animal
form in much the same way as in Ovid's *Metamorphoses*.
The accounts are essentially stories, tales, what the Germans
call *Novellen,* in which the element of historicity as such is of
no significance. As Lesslie Newbigin remarks,

> The care which is taken in the New Testament to place the
> events recorded in the continuum of secular history is in striking
> contrast to the indifference which is generally shown with regard
> to the historicity of the events which Hindu piety loves to remem-

[6] *The Sword and the Flute*, pp. 72f., see also pp. 73–8.
[7] Cf. Thomas, *The Acknowledged Christ*, p. 147.
[8] *The Supernatural Manifestation*, p. 235.
[9] Robert A. McDermott, *Six Pillars: Introductions to the Major Works of Sri
Aurobindo*, p. 168.

ber in connection with the character of the gods. There is no serious attempt to relate them to events in secular history, nor is it felt that there would be any advantage to be gained from trying to do so – even if it could be done. Their value is that they illustrate truths about God which would remain true even if these particular events had not happened.[10]

Sometimes there may indeed be a legendary basis for them (Krishna seems to be a divinized epic hero, a sort of Indian Ulysses), sometimes a historical substratum, or sometimes a clearly defined individual is seen as a manifestation of the divine, such as the Buddha or in more recent times Ramakrishna, Gandhi or any saintly or spiritual man. And among these would certainly be included Jesus, who is honoured among the *illuminati* or God-filled men whose incarnations serve as connecting links of knowledge and grace for the rest of humanity. In Ramakrishna's striking image,

> The incarnation is like a ship which carries innumerable persons to the infinite ocean of God. . . . When a mighty log of wood floats down the stream, it carries on it hundreds of birds and does not sink. . . . So when a Saviour incarnates, innumerable are the men who find salvation by taking refuge in him.[11]

But in the classical conception of the *avatara* he is in no real sense a *product* of the historical process or a fulfilment of it. As my old teacher H. H. Farmer has put it, albeit perhaps too sweepingly, in seeking to distinguish *avatara* from incarnation, he is

> a divine being who merely drops into the historical scene in an embodied form from the realm of eternity, unheralded, unprepared for, without roots in anything that has gone before in history and without any creative relationship to the unfolding of events in what comes after.[12]

That would need some qualification, particularly in regard to Krishna. For in the *Bhagavadgita* his appearance is not unrelated to the state of the world:

[10] *The Finality of Christ*, pp. 52f.

[11] *Sayings of Sri Ramakrishna*, quoted by Swami Akhilananda, *The Hindu View of Christ*, pp. 23f. Cf. Samartha, *The Hindu Response*, pp. 61–72.

[12] *Revelation and Religion*, p. 196; quoted by Parrinder, *Avatar and Incarnation*, p. 119, who lists twelve characteristics of *avatar* doctrines (pp. 120–6).

For whenever the law of righteousness (*dharma*) withers away,
And lawlessness (*adharma*) raises its head,
Then do I generate Myself on earth.

For the protection of the good
For the destruction of evildoers,
For the setting up of righteousness,
I come into being, age after age (4.7 f.).

Yet it is still true that Krishna himself does not enter the fight: his manifestation, in the 'human form I have assumed' (9.11), is to nerve Arjuna to battle; and his divine form and human forms are *alternates* (11.45f., 51f.). In the various stories, which make no claim to be judged or co-ordinated as history, his relationship to the history, let alone the fact of his historicity, is not of itself part of the revelation: he enters the process and passes from it without creating a ripple. 'There is an old Hindu tradition that when an *avatara* walks his feet do not touch the ground so that he leaves no footprints.'[13] Even though he may die, as Krishna does, his death does not affect or effect anything. He is not one of us, an evolved product of the species *homo sapiens*, a man among men who reveals God, but Vishnu making an appearance in the form of a man. And the appearance is all: 'The "body" or human shape assumed is not a real human nature, passible and earthly; it is made of *vishuddha sattva* (heavenly matter), it is a passing manifestation only.'[14]

There is a strong streak in all the stories of what the Christian would recognize as docetism, of the Christ 'seeming' to be a man. And this goes too for the stories of the Buddha, which remind one of the apocryphal rather than of the canonical gospels. Of course the same streak is also to be seen in many of the attempts of the early church fathers to explain the incarnation, especially in the school of Alexandria. Yet always this was recognized as a danger, a tendency to be resisted, and ultimately as heresy to be condemned. But in Buddhism and Hinduism there is no such sense: the more

[13] Boyd, *Indian Christian Theology*, p. 128, interpreting the thought of Bishop A. J. Appasamy (1891–1975), who while prepared to use the *avatara* concept stressed the difference in the reality and historicity of the incarnation of Jesus Christ.

[14] P. Fallon, in *Religious Hinduism*, pp. 253f.

edifying stories there are the better – and often from a moralistic point of view not so edifying. No one is worried (or perhaps one should say almost no one is worried, for there have been somewhat misguided attempts under the impact of the West to rehabilitate the historical Krishna or the Mahabharata war[15]) whether Krishna was *really* like that or stole the butter or lived it up with the milkmaids.[16] It is an allegory of the divine love, on a par with the Song of Songs. As Gandhi said,

> My Krishna has nothing to do with any historical person. . . . I believe in Krishna of my imagination as a perfect incarnation, spotless in every sense of the word;

or again,

> I worship Rama, the perfect being of my conception, not a historical person, facts about whose life may vary with the progress of new historical discoveries and researches.[17]

In fact, 'historical discoveries and researches' have been accorded little serious role in Indian religion. In an important discussion of the status of the historical for Hindu-Christian dialogue Samartha says:

> It is unfortunate that in India not much attention has been given either by Hindu or by Christian writers to understand religious documents *historically*. . . . The absence of a critical attitude towards the texts themselves and the lack of chronological references in some of the major works have not been helpful to develop a positive attitude towards history. Probably with the single exception of Raja Ram Mohan Roy,[18] hardly any Hindu

[15] Cf. Hooker, 'A Disquiet within Hinduism', *New Fire* 4,1976, pp. 146f.; and this from an address given to the Fellowship of St Thomas at Dunblane, Scotland, on 23 September 1978: 'Three years ago a university professor of history wrote an article in which he claimed that the famous Mahabharata war never really happened: "it was only a myth". This provoked a storm of protest from the orthodox. A seminar was held at the Sanskrit University. All the speakers claimed that the war really had taken place. History was real, myth unreal – a very un-Hindu position. Moreover, there was no attempt to discuss the significance of the war. All that mattered was whether "it really happened".'

[16] Cf. Parrinder, *Avatar and Incarnation*, pp. 72–80, 234–7.

[17] *Young India*. 1 October 1925 and 27 August 1925, quoted Parrinder, op. cit., p. 104.

[18] 1772–1833. For his pioneering work cf. Thomas, *The Acknowledged Christ*, ch. 1; Boyd, *Indian Christian Theology*, pp. 19–26.

thinker has given serious attention to the question of historicity
in understanding the life and work of Jesus Christ. Periodically
newspaper statements appear, claiming that Jesus Christ really
did not die on the cross, that he came to Kashmir and died there
and that his tomb is still to be seen in Kashmir. But hardly any
attempt is made to sift facts from myths, real happenings from
wishful thinking.[19]

Gandhi again is typically honest:

> I have never been interested in a historical Jesus. I should not
> care if it was proved by someone that the man called Jesus never
> lived, and that what was narrated in the Gospels was a figment
> of the writer's imagination. For the Sermon on the Mount would
> still be true to me.[20]

Much the same could easily be quoted from other sources.
For example Aurobindo wrote:

> Such controversies as the one that has raged in Europe over the
> historicity of Christ would seem to the spiritually-minded Indian
> largely a waste of time; he would concede to it a considerable
> historical, but hardly any religious importance. If the Christ,
> God made man, lives within our spiritual being, it would seem
> to matter little whether or not a son of Mary physically lived and
> suffered and died in Judea.[21]

Vivekananda in one of his few references to the crucifixion
said:

> Christ was God incarnate; they could not kill him. That which
> was crucified was only a semblance, a mirage.[22]

Similarly Radhakrishnan insisted that:

> Christ is born in the depths of spirit: we say that he passes

[19] *The Hindu Response*, p. 156, cf. pp. 154–62; and earlier *The Hindu View of
History, Classical and Modern*, and 'The Significance of the Historical in Contemporary Hinduism', *IJT* 16, 1967, pp. 95–105.

[20] *The Message of Jesus Christ*, p. 35; quoted Thomas, *The Acknowledged Christ*,
p. 199. Though the crucified Jesus meant much to Gandhi ('When I survey the
wondrous cross' was one of his favourite hymns and sung at his prayer meetings),
the resurrection was completely ignored by him. Cf. Samartha, *The Hindu Response*,
ch. 4, especially pp. 92–6.

[21] *Essays on the Gita*, p. 12.

[22] *Works* I, p. 328, quoted Thomas, *The Acknowledged Christ*, p. 126. I have
altered the style and pagination of his quotations from Vivekananda to conform with
the Mayavati Memorial Edition.

through life, dies on the cross and rises again. Those are not so much historical events which occurred once upon a time as universal processes of spiritual life, which are being continually accomplished in the souls of men.[23]

The resurrection is the uplifting of the human consciousness to the awareness of its true divine nature:[24] 'God descends when man rises.'[25] And the presupposition of this attitude to history, whether of Krishna or Christ, is for him that

the realities of spirit are the same now as they were thousands of years ago . . . The essential thing is truth or significance; and the historical fact is nothing more than the image of it.[26]

In other words, it makes no essential difference to the situation.

Finally, in relation to uniqueness or finality here are two significant quotations which epitomize this whole approach. The first is from Ramakrishna:

It is one and the same Avatara that, having plunged into the ocean of life, rises up in one place and is known as Krishna, and diving again rises in another place and is known as Christ.[27]

The second again is from Vivekananda:

As water in a kettle begins to boil it shows first one bubble, then another, and then more and more till all is ebullition and passes out as steam. Buddha and Christ are the two biggest 'bubbles' the world has yet produced. Moses was a tiny bubble, greater and greater ones came. Sometime however, all will be bubbles and escape; but creation, ever anew, will bring new water to go through the process all over again.[28]

Perhaps I have given the impression that the divide I have been describing coincides too exactly with the line between

---

[23] 'Fragments of a Confession' in *The Philosophy of Sarvepalli Radhakrishnan*, ed. P. A. Schlipp. p. 79; quoted by Thomas, op. cit., p. 154. Cf. Akhilananda, *The Hindu View of Christ*, who similarly regards the events of Christ's life as historical but symbolical, standing for certain universal principles.

[24] Radhakrishnan, *Bhagavadgita*, p. 36.

[25] Ibid., p. 155.

[26] Ibid., p. 37.

[27] Max Muller, *Ramakrishna: His Life and Sayings*, Collected Works XV, p. 109, saying no. 52; quoted by Thomas, op. cit., p. 121.

[28] *Works* VII, pp. 7f.; quoted by Thomas, op. cit., p. 122.

Christianity and Hinduism. But qualifications need to be made from both sides. In a notable essay on 'Indian Theology and the Problem of History' in the *Festschrift* for M. M. Thomas, Fr Samuel Rayan S J has mounted a strong counter-attack on the simplistic notion that Hinduism has a purely cyclical, Christianity a purely linear, idea of history.[29] Neither, he argues, is adequate to the facts or to a true interpretation of the meaning of history. The *Gita* in particular, he says, shows a genuine awareness of history being open to the action of God and of moments and decisions in history mattering. Moreover the sense of history, even in the West, is largely a modern phenomenon: in the Middle Ages 'the historicity of Jesus was taken for granted just as the historicity of Rama and Krishna is taken for granted by the Hindu masses'.[30] The same indeed applies to the understanding of personality[31] and to the scientific attitude to matter, which we shall be considering in the next chapter – though of all three it could truly be said that these were developments implicit in the Judaeo-Christian world-view in the way that they are not in the Hindu or Buddhist. (In fact no other faith – certainly not Islam – has been prepared to submit its own documents to such rigorous historical study as the Christian church.) The modifications cannot undermine the basic distinctions we have been drawing, but they still need making.

Moreover, while it would probably be true to say that Hinduism and Buddhism have traditionally been less sensitive to the place of the historical than to that either of the personal or of the material, things are not static. In conversation I found Hindus wishing to stress that history was processive and spiral rather than purely cyclical and to claim

[29] *Society and Religion*, ed. Richard W. Taylor, pp. 167–93. Cf. also, from Thailand, Kosuke Koyama, *Waterbuffalo Theology*, p. 41: 'The biblical view of history is not circular. It is linear. But life in Thailand is strongly influenced by the circular movement of nature.... Circular nature shows God's glory as much as linear history. Both are purposeful. Yet, as we have seen, circular nature finds its proper place *within* the linear history. In this proper location, circular nature finds its purpose. When two images, circular and linear, are put together, why can we not have the image of an ascending spiral view of one unified history-nature? Is not this image helpful and even necessary in the land of the monsoon orientation? ... Will this not bring the presence of God closer to the people of Thailand?'

[30] *Society and Religion*, p. 180.

[31] Cf. C. C. J. Webb, *God and Personality*.

that, unlike Christians, they believed in an open system with no final term. Even in those who have laid most emphasis on timelessness there is a perceptible shift of emphasis. Thus, as Samartha points out,

> It is significant that in his latest book Radhakrishnan, for the first time in all his writings, has found it necessary to write a separate chapter on 'The Meaning of History'.[32] Advaita can no longer be accused of being indifferent to the problems of the world.[33]

And it is for this reason, precisely 'when increasing attention is being paid to the historical in Hinduism', that he, as an Indian Christian theologian, is anxious that 'ontological concern does not swallow up the historical fact of Jesus Christ.'[34] Similarly, Thomas in a chapter headed significantly 'Buddhist Messianism and Existential Suffering' notes how 'the Convocation of the Sixth Buddhist Council in Rangoon was linked with the Buddhist expectation of "the coming of a new Buddha" ', the fifth and last, 'whose coming is nigh'.[35] This eschatological note is associated with a new involvement in politics especially in South-East Asia, and, as we ourselves saw in Sri Lanka, expresses itself in a communalism which is by no means always universalist or pacific. The lotus is unfolding.

Furthermore, I detect on the other side not only a strong element in classical Christianity and Western mysticism which would subordinate the historical to the timeless – 'There is no greater obstacle to God than time' (Eckhart)[36] – but a marked modern protest against its overvaluation. In all the recent turning towards Eastern religions, meditation and yoga there is a distinct turning away from any kind of exclusive historical claims or Protestant particularism, and in the renewed awareness, especially through Jungian psychology, of the importance of myth and archetype there is a new

---

[32] *Religion in a Changing World*, ch. 7.
[33] *The Hindu Response*, p. 165; cf. also his *Introduction to Radhakrishnan*, ch. 5, and his essay, 'Major Issues in Hindu-Christian Dialogue in India Today', in *Inter-Religious Dialogue*, ed. H. Jai Singh, pp. 166–9.
[34] *The Hindu Response*, p. 141. He criticizes Panikkar's *Unknown Christ of Hinduism* for being open to this interpretation in a Hindu context.
[35] *Man and the Universe of Faiths*, p. 80. Cf. E. Benz, *Buddhism or Communism*.
[36] Quoted by Otto, *Mysticism East and West*, p. 66.

readiness to detach the Christ-figure from more than a minimal dependence on the Jesus of history. And this has been powerfully reinforced by the conclusion of certain schools of historical criticism that there is not much that can be said about the Jesus of history anyhow. As one who has recently put a good deal of time and trouble into a book called *Redating the New Testament*, in which I argue on historico-critical grounds for a much shorter gap than scholars have recently supposed between the person and the records, I can hear in the comments of many of my friends, admittedly in less extreme form, the reaction of Vivekananda:

> It does not matter at all whether the New Testament was written within five hundred years of his birth, nor does it matter, even, how much of that life is true. But there is something behind it, something we want to imitate.[37]

This protest is a healthy reminder that all the truth about history and the Christ does not lie on one side. Indeed, as in the first lecture, I should wish to say that each pole when seen as the centre of a self-contained isolated circle produces a serious distortion of the truth. So let me sketch two contrasting caricatures, not accusing anyone on either side of actually holding them, but seeing them as warnings of what can happen when a one-eyed view takes over.

The distorting effects

On the one hand, we have a historical positivism or fundamentalism of an all-or-nothing kind, which lacks discrimination, self-criticism and above all imagination. At its best it is pedestrian, at its worst blinkered and dismissive. It operates with hard edges and enjoys a 'laager' mentality. It glories in intolerance and in believing *because* it is absurd. It asks with Tertullian, 'What is there in common between Athens and Jerusalem?' – or for that matter between Delhi and Jerusalem. It preaches a Christ who is exclusive rather than inclusive, attaching the narrowest and most negative interpretation to biblical texts which suggest that there is salvation in no other

---

[37] *Works* IV, p. 146; quoted by Thomas, op. cit., p. 121.

name. It links redemption to a transaction made two thousand years ago which it tends to isolate from all that led up to it and from all that has flowed from it. It has no problems with the relation between the Christ of faith and the Jesus of history for they are viewed uncritically as one and the same, and everything he said and did is to be accepted and interpreted quite literally.

In Western Europe and North America this unlovely thing is largely now an Evangelical and sectarian phenomenon, but until recently historical triumphalism, extending beyond the Bible to the church and papacy, was as characteristic of main line Catholic Christianity. In other forms of Protestantism the mirror-image has taken the form of a 'historicism', which again creates an 'ism' of history, ironically by absolutizing the relativities of history: there is no criterion beyond history by which to judge history. The exaltation of the historical as an end in itself has led also outside the church to rationalist doctrines of secular progress and in Marxism to dialectical materialism. Harnessed to the capitalist and scientific revolutions, whose link with the biblical doctrine of creation must engage us later, it has produced the technocratic imperialism which has ravaged the Western, and now not only the Western, way of life. It threatens the environment of the whole biosphere.

It has been claimed by a World Council of Churches report that while 'in ancient religions, history is naturalized, in Israel, nature is historicized'.[38] But the historicizing of nature destroys it as nature, as modern Israel as well as much of the rest of the globe shows. And making an 'ism' or idol of history does violence not only to nature but to man – hence the pressures in the over-historicized West to return to the rhythms of more 'natural' and organic living. Finally, in the third world, as Rayan points out, by the test of praxis,

> it will not do merely to assert that the consciousness of world history, and the forces that 'have transformed all previous history into world history', stem from the Christian faith and have roots

---

[38] *New Directions in Faith and Order*, p. 10; quoted by Samartha, *Hindu Response*, pp. 174f.

in the historicness and universality of the Christian idea of God[39] ... It is not easy for Asia and Africa and for the wretched of the earth anywhere to associate 'historicness and universality' with the God-idea which can co-exist with a practice of history in terms of colonial mastery, white overlordship, military-capitalist oligarchies, and racism and apartheid and in terms of used and neglected hungry human masses.[40]

On the other hand, the East at its worst (but not the East only, for there are parallels, in the West, especially in an individualistic, other-worldly and supposedly unpoliticized but in fact reactionary piety)[41] has been characterized by a dangerous historical absenteeism, making for a quietist indifference and fatalistic irresponsibility. It has shown itself lacking muscle for economic reform or leverage for political change. Without faith in a God going on before, calling out, charging the future with significance and hope, it has not been change-ful. With no sense of man's delegated lordship over history, it has resigned itself to having little purchase over events or power to affect the *karma* of groups or individuals.[42] The subordination of human beings and their purposes to the cycle of nature ('Like corn a man grows up, like corn he's born again')[43] is caricatured for the West by the phenomenon of the sacred cow, which even Gandhi was to defend as 'the central fact of Hinduism'. Persons and particulars get swamped and submerged, and that not simply by the uncontrolled flood of numbers. For if 'history is essentially the sphere of the singular, the unique',[44] if one of its characteristics is that it does not repeat itself, then any teaching of

---

[39] So W. Pannenberg, *Basic Questions in Theology* 1, p. 69 n. 136.

[40] *Society and Religion*, ed. Richard W. Taylor, pp. 192f.

[41] The groundswell of approval in conservative church circles for the 1978 Reith Lectures by Edward R. Norman, *Christianity and World Order*, was more significant than the content of the lectures themselves.

[42] Cf. Swami Nikhilananda: 'India wants to make good her escape from the ties imposed by nature through a loop-hole by means of renunciation. The method of the West has been to expand itself more and more so that nature will not find a rope long enough to bind her', *Western Mechanism and Hindu Mysticism*, p. 24. He defends 'the much-criticized caste system' as 'the best social system ever evolved by human mind to eliminate friction from society' (p. 30). Note that he says 'friction' rather than 'injustice'.

[43] *Katha Up. 1.6.1.*

[44] Cf. Farmer, *Revelation and Religion*, pp. 195f.

virtually endless reincarnations (by traditional computation 8,400,000) or of release from them into a timeless *nirvana* must inevitably have the effect of lessening the decisiveness and cutting the nerve of historical involvement.

It also has the remarkable consequence for a Westerner which comes out in the Japanese capacity for 'forgetting' history, for instance, in wiping the slate clean after 1945 and beginning again.[45] As a Japanese Christian, K. T. Chou, has observed,[46] the forgetting rather than the forgiving of resentment is a characteristic of Buddhist teaching: 'History can be washed away.' Yet, as she acknowledges with reference to atrocities like the Burma Road, 'only the Japanese forget': 'There is a lack of awareness of history as vital decision, and this leads to a type of historical irresponsibility.'[47]

Of course all this has been far from the full picture, and both Buddhism and Hinduism have inspired much compassion for humanity and social concern. To this I shall return in the next chapter. Yet in the course of analysing the current revolution in Asia, M. M. Thomas notes four emerging characteristics, all associated with an awakening to a sharpened sense of the personal and historical. In summary these are: (1) the distinctiveness of man from nature in his essential being; (2) the ultimate core of the individual's responsibility and his right to nonconformity; (3) the conviction that institutions, communal and religious, are 'made for man' in a free and equal association of persons; and (4) the awareness of a goal, a future, for society in which alienations can and must be reconciled in love and justice.[48] It is, however, significant that these are discussed in a chapter called 'The search for *new* spiritual foundations'. The stabilities of the traditional

[45] Cf. the brilliant assessment of the Japanese character which Ruth Benedict, the American sociologist, was commissioned to prepare towards the end of World War II by the US authorities, *The Chrysanthemum and the Sword*. Despite the fact that she had never been to Japan when she wrote it, it was recommended to us by the Japanese themselves as the best introduction for a Westerner. The phenomenon of 'burying' history is connected with her characterization of Japanese society as a shame-culture rather than a guilt-culture (pp. 222–4).

[46] 'Christian Dialogue with Traditional Japanese Culture', *The Japan Christian Quarterly* 44, 1978, pp. 5–11.

[47] Op. cit., p. 11.

[48] *The Christian Response to the Asian Revolution*, pp. 67f.

Asian cultures, so far from promoting them, are seen as rendering them problematic. A feel for the distinctive values of
the historical and personal is not native or automatic to this
way of thinking.

Reference to the current social and political scene is a
reminder that the holding together of both poles, whatever
the tensions it produces and is producing, is not merely a
matter of theory but of pressing practical relevance. And this
is true not only for the East. Western historicism, especially
under the form of secularism, which means making an 'ism'
or god of this *saeculum* or age, is equally destructive of a
truly personal community and spirituality: man is torn apart
between individualism and collectivism and there is a sensed
loss of 'soul' (it is interesting how the category has returned
in non-religious speech) both in politics and in man's relationship to the totality of his environment.

The eternal in the temporal

But at this point I should like to come back to the issue of
historicity. For the question of a historical faith and of the
relation of the Christ, the manifestation and meeting of the
divine in the human, to the datable, tangible actualities of
historical existence, is ultimately of profound significance for
faith *in* history and its meaning. It is also the point at which
the prophetic and the mystical traditions tend to be most
sharply divided. Rightly or wrongly, the first and most insidi-
ous challenge to Christianity was sensed to come from the
Gnostics, whose denial of 'Christ come in the flesh' appeared
to the writer of the Johannine Epistles (I John 2.22; 4.3; II
John 7) as very 'antichrist', the ultimate denial of history as
God-filled.

Perhaps then one could focus this issue by viewing it
through the eyes of this man, who I believe to be the same as
the author of the Fourth Gospel (or is in any case so closely
associated with him as for our purposes to make no difference). For the Gospel of John, taken with his Epistles, is a
good test-case of interpretation, just as the *Bhagavadgita* has
served as a litmus test of interpretation for the different

schools of Hinduism. The first commentaries on the Fourth
Gospel were written by the Gnostics and it has been the one,
what Clement of Alexandria called the 'spiritual gospel',
which has always appealed instinctively to those of this tend-
ency. This has been true also for the Greek mind generally,
and for the Eastern. A symposium has recently appeared on
*India's Search for Reality and the Relevance of the Gospel of
St John*, [49] and there is actually a book called *The Christian
Buddhism of St John* by a Canadian Roman Catholic monk,
J. Edgar Bruns, who believes, I think quite improbably, that
John was directly influenced by Buddhist thought. Similarly
Abhishiktananda spoke of 'the Johannine Upanishads', [50]
though he could do this only by isolating the prologue and
the last discourses from the body of the gospel narrative and
from the historicity of the Christ-events, an issue which
remarkably plays no part in his *Hindu-Christian Meeting
Point*. The parallels especially between the prologue to the
Fourth Gospel and the Upanishads have fascinated many,
both Christian and Hindu, not least the inspirer of the Teape
Lectures, Bishop Westcott. His judgment that 'the most profound commentary on the Fourth Gospel was still to be written, and that it could not be written until an Indian theologian
would undertake the task' is quoted on the first page of Robin
Boyd's *Introduction to Indian Christian Theology*. Actually
it is a sentiment which I would beg leave to doubt until India
shows more signs of coming to terms with the fact, which
modern scholarship is I believe beginning to recognize, that
this Gospel is not only the most theological but may also, in
its profound concern for the Word made flesh, be the most
truly historical of the four.

Certainly within Hinduism itself little attempt has been
made to wrestle with this aspect of it. Characteristic was the
purely gnosticizing interpretation of it that came into my
hands in Bangalore, from a syncretistic group of Hindus and
Sikhs, by Maharaj Charan Singh, *St John the Great Mystic*.

---

[49] Edited by C. Duraisingh and C. Hargreaves. Duraisingh's own contribution,
'The Gospel of John and the World of India Today', pp. 41–55, is a powerful blast
against any attempt to detach this gospel from the world of history and social change.

[50] *Hindu-Christian Meeting Point*, ch. 6.

It was a commentary on the first seventeen chapters, ignoring
the death and resurrection of Christ entirely, and isolating
the prologue and selected sayings from the narrative. Typically it made no attempt to get to the original historical
meaning.

At a more sophisticated level one could quote Vivekan-
ananda, who believed that the whole essence of Christianity was
contained in the first five verses of the prologue. Here is his
comment on the first:

> 'In the beginning was the Word, and the Word was with God,
> and the Word was God.' The Hindu calls this Maya, the man-
> ifestation of God, because it is the power of God. . . . The Word
> has two manifestations – the general one of nature, and the
> special one of the great Incarnations of God – Krishna, Buddha,
> Jesus, and Ramakrishna. Christ, the special manifestation of the
> Absolute, is known and knowable. The Absolute cannot be
> known: we cannot know the Father, only the Son. We can only
> see the Absolute through the 'tint of humanity', through Christ.[51]

But this manifestation, he says, implies neither uniqueness
nor finality:

> In time to come Christs will be in numbers like bunches of grapes
> on a vine; then the play will be over and will pass out.[52]

And he proceeds to use the analogy I cited earlier of a series
of bubbles appearing and evaporating, on which M. M. Thomas comments:

> It is clear that even the purpose of the Divine Incarnations is to
> help the water become bubbles and escape, to help liberation
> from the total complex of the manifestations of Maya, including
> world history and personality through the Advaitic vision that
> God alone is.[53]

Now it is safe to say that whatever else St John meant he

---

[51] *Works* VII, p. 3.
[51] *Works* VII, p. 7.
[53] *The Acknowledged Christ*, p. 122. For a fuller assessment, cf. J. R. Chandran,
*Christian Apologetics in Relation to Vivekananda in the Light of Origen, Contra
Celsum*, unpublished B.Litt. thesis at Oxford, cited extensively by Thomas, op. cit.,
pp. 129–38.

did not mean this.[54] Indeed it is very near to what, as I read it, he sees the gnosticizing false teachers have made of him, teachers against whom he reacts so vehemently in the Epistles. For they have apparently interpreted him as commending an undifferentiated God-mysticism whose ultimate goal is to 'have the Father without the Son'. This has the effect not only of denying the flesh of Christ in a docetic understanding of the incarnation and the cross (he came 'without the blood'), but of repudiating the material needs of the brother. Who, he asks, can love God whom he has not seen if he loves not his brother whom he has seen (I John 4.20–5.12)? So he is led in the opening verse of the first Epistle to stress uncompromisingly the reality of what 'we have heard, we have seen with our own eyes and felt with our own hands' (I John 1.1). And this reads like a preliminary sketch for the prologue to the Gospel, which was added later, I believe,[55] to set the history in cosmic perspective and to stress from the beginning the inescapable significance of the Word become *flesh*.

The relation of the Fourth Gospel to history presents a fascinating paradox. On the one hand, it appears, and has been appraised as, the most Gnostic of the gospels. Yet it can hardly be accidental that all the favourite Gnostic terms are missing from it: *gnosis* (knowledge), *sophia* (wisdom), even *pistis* (faith), together with others like 'revelation' and 'mystery' and, in a technical sense, *pleroma* (fullness), all of which St Paul seems deliberately to use to turn against his opponents. St John is so near, and yet so far. Again he has frequently been understood by distinguished interpreters, ancient and modern,[56] as presenting a divine Christ walking this earth in the semblance of a man before returning whence he came – the very *avatara* figure seen in him by Hindus and Buddhists and even, as far as the cross is concerned, by Muslims, whose Koran denies the reality of his death. Yet no

[54] It is ironic that Vivekananda accused the West of 'text-torturing', with the splendid remark: 'Texts are not India rubber, and even that has its limits' (*Works* IV, p. 144).
[55] 'The Relation of the Prologue to the Gospel of St. John', *New Testament Studies*, 9, 1962–63, pp. 120–9.
[56] Most recently by E. Käsemann, *The Testament of Jesus*.

one stresses more than John the sheer physical factuality of
Jesus' death:

> When they came to Jesus, they found that he was already dead,
> so they did not break his legs. But one of the soldiers stabbed his
> side with a lance, and at once there was a flow of blood and
> water. This is vouched for by an eyewitness, whose evidence is
> to be trusted. He knows that he speaks the truth (19.33–35).

When confronted, as we have seen, with a docetic construc-
tion put upon his message, he recoils in horror. Again, the
Fourth Gospel has been dismissed as the least historical of
the four, interested solely in a timeless mystical Christ and
far removed in space and time from the events it records. Yet
actually it contains a great many more indications of place
and time than the others, and its details both of topography
and chronology are increasingly coming to be vindicated in
recent study. Indeed I am now persuaded that it is in every
sense a primitive gospel, going back very near to source,
though *also* the most mature penetration of the spiritual and
theological truth of the history it presents: the alpha as well
as the omega of the New Testament witness.[57]

So let us take it as a paradigm of how the historical and
the eternal, the prophetic and the mystical, may be held
together without loss or absorption of either.

Despite the fact that John has also been seized on by the
fundamentalists (it is their favourite gospel too – or rather
texts from it!), it is the least hospitable to historicism, or to
historicity for its own sake: 'the flesh' *per se* 'is of no avail'
(6.63). Nor, though this again has been claimed for it, does
it really afford any basis for an exclusivist Christ. But treatment of this I shall reserve for chapter 5. It is, of course, like
all the gospels, primarily concerned to present the Christ of
faith. The verse quoted above, 'He knows that he speaks the
truth', goes on 'so that you too may *believe*' (19.35), and this
is reaffirmed in the concluding statement of the Gospel's
purpose (20.31). But the point is that for John, as again for
all the evangelists, the Christ of faith *includes* the Jesus of

[57] Until I can write more fully on this, I must be content to refer in justification
to *Redating the New Testament*, ch. 9.

history. The flesh is as important as the Word. This is not to say that they can simply be identified in an uncritical or fundamentalist way. Indeed John is projecting, as it were, two colour transparencies, one on top of the other. It is possible to see simply what the eyes see, and, like most of 'the Jews' in this Gospel, to see no more than a rabbi from Nazareth. Or it is possible simply to see the divine Christ, as many subsequent interpreters have done, Christian as well as Hindu. Or it is possible, like Nicodemus, to get the two hopelessly confused and to take literally statements about the history that are there to disclose its ultimate, spiritual significance. Or it is possible, in the 'true' light (1.9), to see the 'glory' *in* the 'flesh' (1.14), the divine form (in contrast with the *Gita*) *in* the human. John's purpose is to show the truth, the real meaning entered into, *of* the history. For this eyewitness is vital, and it matters profoundly if it never happened or was quite different. But he can still treat his material with sovereign freedom, for it is only in 'spirit' (and 'in the Spirit') and not at the level of 'flesh' that it can truly be apprehended. It is not accuracy (*akribeia*) that he is primarily interested in (that is a Lukan concern) but truth *(aletheia)*, not psychological verisimilitude but theological verity, especially in interpreting the words and works of Jesus. The Christ speaks and acts from beyond the purely historical. Yet the happenedness, in our history, is of the essence of the matter.[58]

Paul Tillich, a theologian with great respect both for Platonic philosophy and for Eastern religion,[59] and in my judgment unduly distrustful of historical research to provide a foundation for faith, nevertheless recognized in Jesus what he called 'the fresh colours of a life really lived'. 'It was just this concreteness and incomparable uniqueness', he said, 'of the "real" picture which gave Christianity its superiority over mystery cults and Gnostic visions.'[60] And he could have added, as Parrinder did when he quoted this in his *Avatar*

---

[58] Cf. at fuller length my contribution, 'The Use of the Fourth Gospel for Christology Today', to the *Festschrift* for C. F. D. Moule, *Christ and Spirit in the New Testament*, edited by B. Lindars and S. S. Smalley, pp. 61–78.

[59] Cf. especially his *Christianity and the Encounter of the World Religions*.

[60] *Systematic Theology* II, Nisbet 1957, p. 174; SCM Press 1978, p. 151.

and Incarnation,[61] over the stories of Hinduism and Buddhism, as indeed over the apocryphal in contrast with the canonical gospels. It is undeniable that there is legend, symbolism and myth in the gospels, and there will continue to be divergence over what is to be taken at what level. But these are there not to displace the history but to interpret, to draw out the ultimate divine significance of, the history. There is no reason for, and every reason against, giving to this history an all-or-nothing uniqueness which suggests that *as history* it is different from any other history or which excludes revelation or salvation elsewhere. That was never the way of the early Christian apologists like Clement and Origen, also great interpreters of the Fourth Gospel, who saw the *Logos* at work universally. Yet, as Augustine said of the Platonists of his day, what he did not find in them was that the Word was made *flesh*.[62]

Yet we do justice to this distinctive contribution from the Hebraic side not by isolating the Christ-event as an exception, glorying in its anomaly, but by seeing it in A. N. Whitehead's phrase, as the 'supreme exemplification', the normative expression, of the relation between the Word and the world, *Brahman* and *maya,* Reality and *samsara.* As I shall be exploring further in the last two chapters, I believe that if the affirmation of incarnation – and I would prefer this to the isolating term 'the Incarnation' with a definite article and capital letter[63]–can be seen in the East no longer as a threat nor, as in some recent theological circles in the West, as an embarrassment to be shed, then there is a hope as never before of a much broader-based Christology in the proper sense of that word – a *logos* not simply about Jesus but about *Christos.* We can begin to work through together to what it means to say that history is charged with divine significance.

For this the mystical centre needs the prophetic centre if it is not to become airborne. Writing of Aurobindo, among the most open of the mystics to the horizontal movement of evolution, one of his most sympathetic critics questions

---

[61] *Avatar and Incarnation,* pp. 236f.
[62] *Confessions* 7.9.1f.
[63] *The Human Face of God,* pp. 230–6.

whether he can escape the charge of 'vapid spiritualism' and 'idealistic utopianism'.[64] And this may not be entirely unconnected with the fact, as another admirer confesses, that, despite his Western education,

> it must be said that nowhere in his writings does Sri Aurobindo show any depth of appreciation for the Christian mysteries, Christian spirituality or Christian culture,

and indeed that

> the entire sequence of his studies on Indian culture is weakened considerably by constant derogatory references to the spiritual and religious aspects of Western culture.[65]

Despite his Cambridge education, his parochialism is very marked compared, say, with Radhakrishnan, who was mentally a citizen of the world. But equally the prophetic centre needs the mystical centre if it is not to become arrogant, narrow and unlovely – all that E. M. Forster caricatured in his *Passage to India*[66] as 'poor little talkative Christianity'.

Nowhere, I suggested earlier, is the gulf of mutual understanding between the two 'eyes' perhaps greater than in the estimate of the historical. I have deliberately cited men like Gandhi and Aurobindo because they have taken most from the West and, in the case of the former, from Christianity. But Gandhi's great friend C. F. Andrews confessed that he never felt that the Mahatma got through to the person of Christ as opposed to the principles of Christ. And his interpreter E. Stanley Jones wrote similarly in a letter to him:

> May I suggest that you penetrate through the principles to the Person and then come back and tell us what you have found? I don't say this as a mere Christian propagandist. I say this because we need you and need the illustration you could give us if you really grasped the centre – the Person.[67]

---

[64] J. Bruce Long, in *Six Pillars*, edited by Robert A. McDermott, p. 126.

[65] Thomas Berry in *Six Pillars*, pp. 40f.

[66] *Passage to India*, p. 157 (the last paragraph of ch. 14).

[67] *Mahatma Ghandi: An Interpretation*, p. 80; quoted Thomas, *Salvation and Humanisation*, p. 33, who argues the need for a theology of mission in contemporary India which digs into the Principle itself for the acknowledgement of the Person implicit within it.

'Indeed', says Thomas again,

> the crucial issue in the theological debate between Christians
> and Gandhi is whether the historical Person of Jesus Christ is an
> essential part of the Christian kerygma, or whether his signifi-
> cance for the life of mankind was exhausted by being accepted
> and assimilated as the supreme symbol of the principle of
> redemptive love.[68]

There is here, he believes, an either-or decision to be taken.
Moreover he sees strongly the connection between the historicity of Jesus and the whole concern for 'humanisation'
which he has made his own:

> Probably one of the most important tasks of a theology of mission
> is to restate the significance of the historicity of the Person of
> Jesus within the essential core of the Christian message. It is
> only if a historical event belongs to the essence of the Christian
> Gospel that historical human existence can acquire a positive
> relation to our eternal salvation.[69]

And interestingly he lays his primary stress on a point on
which Gandhi and the rest lay least:

> the bodily resurrection of Jesus as a happening in secular history.
> Of course one could be as sophisticated as one wants with regard
> to the definition of the term 'bodily', with respect to the nature
> of the spiritual body of the Risen Jesus and its relation to the
> mortal body before death. But man is a bodily being and it is
> this that makes him a historical being. The question whether the
> ultimate spiritual destiny of man involves a redemption and
> consummation of his history is ultimately based on the resurrec-
> tion of Jesus being a bodily one – being a _happenedness_ with
> some deposit in the chronological history, and not only in some
> primal salvation history known only to God and faith or only in
> the history of the internal soul of individual believers.[70]

In a different way Bede Griffiths, who is strongly on the
advaitic side and yet has a keen sense of the importance of
history, poses the same issue. Comparing Krishna and Christ
he says:

---

[68] _The Acknowledged Christ_, p. 235. Cf. also Nirmal Minz, _Mahatma Gandhi
and Hindu-Christian Dialogue._
[69] _Salvation and Humanisation_, p. 29.
[70] Ibid., p. 30.

Christianity also has a place for an ideal love, which is joyous
and ecstatic. . . . Has Hinduism also a place for a God who
suffers and dies on the cross, for a God who enters history, for
a love which is experienced in the midst of suffering and dereliction? That, perhaps, is the crucial question.[71]

Nothing is gained by burking the historical issue. Yet I believe
that where the greatest tension is there also is the possibility
of the greatest creativity. I am persuaded that in the new
interface both with Eastern mysticism and with Jungian psychology (where Christ crucified and risen is seen as the profoundest image of the archetype of the self) there is greater
hope for fresh light on Christology, again in the widest sense
of that word, than at any time since the classical debates of
the fourth and fifth centuries. But we shall receive this further
illumination neither by soft-pedalling the historical nor by
selling short the claims of divine incarnation. Rather it is by
having a high doctrine of both. And in the long run this
theological debate, about the significance of the flesh for the
divine, is far from irrelevant, as I have indicated, to the social
and political meaning to be discerned in man's entire historical existence and destiny.

But conversely, as Rayan insists, in his plea for a Christology not of

the India of the past, of the Rishis and the Upanishads, but the
India of today, of the factories, five year plans and atomic reac-
tors, . . . emphasis on the historical should be made meaningful
by showing in relief the significance of Jesus for society and social
change. Otherwise situating Jesus in history becomes unimpor-
tant, and history fails to enter truly into the heart of religion.[72]

And that leads directly into the closely related theme of our
next chapter, 'Man and the Material'.

---

[71] *Return to the Centre*, p. 83.
[72] 'Interpreting Christ to India Today: The Contribution of the Roman Catholic
Seminaries', *IJT* 23, 1974, pp. 229–31. (The author's name is here spelt 'Ryan'.)

CHAPTER IV

Man and the Material

Two valuations of matter

In our look so far at the two ways of viewing reality which as a very rough generalization could be called the Hebraic and the Hindu, the prophetic and the mystical, we have focused on their understandings of God and the personal and of the Christ and the historical.

Now I turn to that aspect of reality which may be summed up under the heading 'man and the material'. This is intimately connected with the other two, particularly the latter. For, as Thomas said, 'man is a bodily being and it is this that makes him a historical being'. Taking history seriously means taking matter seriously. In a pamphlet written shortly before he died in 1944, called *What Christians Stand for in the Secular World*, William Temple, then Archbishop of Canterbury, spoke of two interlocking commitments, 'decision for the God who acts' and 'decision for neighbour'. That is to say, he joined response to the God of history with commitment to persons in their material environment. He was also well-known for his remark that Christianity is 'the most avowedly materialist of all the great religions'.[1] So let us look again at the polarity from this point of view, attempting sympathetically to enter into what each centre stands for, observing the distortions when either becomes isolated from the other, and then trying to see how both together in their strength and

[1] *Nature, Man and God*, p. 478.

distinctiveness, rather than by dilution or absorption, can lead to a richer and more creative complex.

Beginning as we have previously from the Hebraic-prophetic end, which is predominantly the centre from which I start, the fundamental affirmation here is that 'God saw everything that he had made, and behold, it was very good' (Gen. 1.31). Its doctrine of creation, all commentators agree, is one of the characteristic and distinctive features of the Jewish-Christian world-view compared with the Hindu-Buddhist. It is a world-affirming approach, in which matter is in no sense illusory or inferior. It is neither divinized nor is it regarded as unreal or evil. The material order is not an emanation of Spirit *from* which it is necessary to turn or return in order to find God, but a positive expression of his will *in* which he is to be met and obeyed. And man is called to share in the divine creativity, in this freedom over nature out of which he comes. Yet it is a dominion tied to responsibility for it, summed up in the relationship of stewardship.

There is general agreement too that this relative 'over-againstness' of man to nature has not only been the source of the distinctive sense of history in the Hebraeo-Christian tradition but a potent factor in the development of modern science from the seventeenth century onwards. It is no accident that this was historically and geographically a brain-child of the Christian West[2] – though Arabic influences, still from the same matrix of thought, must not be underestimated.[3] The harnessing of matter and power in technology, the prising open of the forces of nature for the service of man, are consistent expressions of this attitude, just as the use of money to make money in the capitalist revolution has been shown to be strongly rooted in the religion and ethic of the Protestant Reformation.[4] The rise of liberal bourgeois democracy, too, and of secularization, which as a neutral process is to be distinguished from secular*ism* and represents a proper liberation of life from religious and metaphysical control, are

[2] Cf. I. G. Barbour, *Issues in Science and Religion*, pp. 45–8, and the references there given, especially to Whitehead and to the articles of M. B. Foster.

[3] Cf. the references in Thomas, *Man and the Universe of Faiths*, p. 97.

[4] Classically articulated in R. H. Tawney, *Religion and the Rise of Capitalism*.

equally evident fruits of this basic assessment of man's purchase over nature to shape and order his own destiny. The
instrumental 'I-it' relationship of observation, analysis and
manipulation is a function of the 'I-Thou' relationship, in
which duality is not swallowed up in identity.

But the prophetic tradition, as I said, never allows man to
escape from the fact that he is not merely responsible for but
responsible to – and that both to God and to neighbour:
'Adam, where art thou?' (Gen. 3.9), 'Cain, where is thy
brother Abel?' (Gen. 4.9). It is this dimension of addressa-
bility and answerability in which the whole of life has to be
lived, and out of which ultimately none can fall, that is the
distinctive meaning of man's creation in God's image.[5] He
has to reflect, to give back, the word that God speaks to him.
This was the burden of the Hebrew prophets, of Amos, Hosea
and Isaiah, whose teaching was to be summarized by Micah
in the familiar words: 'And what does the Lord require of you
but to do justice, and to love kindness, and to walk humbly
with your God?' (Micah 6.8). And the point is that this
spiritual question cannot be answered except through the
material and the political. Listen to Jeremiah addressing the
ne'er-do-well son of Josiah, who succeeded him as king of
Judah:

> Woe to him who builds his house by unrighteousness, and his
> upper rooms by injustice; who makes his neighbour serve him
> for nothing, and does not give him his wages; who says 'I will
> build myself a great house with spacious upper rooms', and cuts
> out windows for it, panelling it with cedar, and painting it with
> vermilion. Do you think you are a king because you compete in
> cedar? Did not your father . . . do justice and righteousness?
> Then it was well with him. He judged the cause of the poor and
> needy. . . . *Is not this to know me? says the Lord* (Jer. 22.13–16).

Right politics *is* religion: it is what to know the God of history
means.[6] He is to be met and responded to not by turning
one's back on the world but, in Buber's phrase, '*between* man
and man' or, in Bonhoeffer's, as 'the beyond *in* the midst'.

---

[5] See E. Brunner, *Man in Revolt*, especially ch. 5.
[6] Cf. more fully my *On Being the Church in the World*, ch. 8.

The New Testament reinforces this understanding of God and the material order by its radical doctrine of the incarnation or 'enfleshment' of the Word. There is no need to look away from earth to be shown the Father (John 14.7–10). He may be seen, heard and handled in a man of flesh and blood, who is to him 'as an only son to his father' (John 1.14). St John's words are a metaphor from human relationships, not an exclusive metaphysical statement. For it is not only in this man, as if he were, as I put it before, an anomalous exception, that the divine image is to be seen. He is the supreme exemplification or focal point of what should be true of every son of God.[7] For according to the New Testament itself the Christ is to be met and responded to not simply in the individual Jesus but in the least of his brethren. To have ministered to the sick, fed the hungry, clothed the naked, visited the prisoner, is to have ministered – or not to have ministered – to *him* (Matt. 25.31–46).

Consequently the religion of incarnation is committed through and through to a sacramental understanding of the world. Henceforth nothing can be called common or unclean (Acts. 11.8f). It is in this sense that it is the most avowedly materialist of the great religions, not because it encourages material*ism*, which represents the valuation and validation of matter as an end in itself, what Paul calls 'the mind (or outlook) of the flesh', which cannot know God (Rom. 8.7f), but because it sees matter as holy, as the body of Christ. Its central act of worship, the eucharist, focuses upon samples of matter, bread and wine, and their taking, blessing, breaking and sharing to be the carriers of Christ's transforming life to the world. The 'doing' of this is inescapably too a piece of social action. The holy community there recreated is the pattern, pledge and instrument of all society made new in the kingdom of God.[8] There is a straight line through from here to the social gospel, to the struggle between what Berdyaev called 'the divine mystery of bread and the demonic mystery of money'. Hence the contemporary flowering of prophetic

[7] On this see further ch. 5 below.
[8] For an expansion of this, cf. again my *On Being the Church in the World*, ch. 3, and *Liturgy Coming to Life*.

religion in such movements as liberation theology, black theology and women's theology. And it should come as no surprise to find that one of the most acclaimed productions of the first of these is a volume called *Marx and the Bible* by José Miranda. One-sided it may be, but it *is* one side. No one would write a book on Marx and the Vedas except to contrast their social and political effects, as indeed Marx himself did in his writings on India.[9] Yet before leaving this prophetic centre I would stress that its very concern for matter is ultimately spiritual. Perhaps this can be expressed in two further remarks from theologians I have already quoted. First, Temple's lesser known observation on Marxist dialectical materialism, that 'its own dialectic will destroy its character as materialist';[10] and secondly, Berdyaev's pregnant paradox, 'Bread for myself is a material problem; bread for other people is a spiritual problem.'

But let us now turn to the other centre and see how things look from there, remembering once again that this is in no sense simply an either-or between East and West or a line-up of Hinduism and Buddhism against Judaism and Christianity. For its more negative evaluation of matter is to be found almost as strongly in Christianity, especially in the ascetical and mystical traditions, just as many correctives to its exclusive emphasis are to be found within the Eastern religions. But first let us view it in its own positive strength.

The starting point here is attachment to the inner spiritual centre and a corresponding detachment from the outer and the material, not as evil but as *maya*. This again, as Hindu philosophers like Ramanuja and Madhva and more recently Radhakrishnan have been at pains to stress, does not mean illusion as such (though Shankara certainly compared it to a mirage in the desert or to the optical illusion of taking a coiled rope for a snake),[11] but relative unreality, contingent being,

[9] R. Palme Dutt gives a resumé of these in his *India Today*, pp. 95f. Cf. Thomas, *The Christian Response to the Asian Revolution*, p. 15.

[10] *Nature, Man and God*, p. 488.

[11] Cf. Zaehner, *Mysticism Sacred and Profane*, p. 143: 'Those who are new to Shankara's conception of *maya* or "illusion" seem to doubt whether he really means what he says. He does.' Yet cf. M. Hiriyanna, *Outlines of Indian Philosophy*, pp. 351–3.

which if taken for the real or necessary being is delusion.[12] As Panikkar puts it, *maya* begins by meaning

> the mysterious power, wisdom or skill of the Gods, hence the power of deceit, illusion. In Vedanta it is used as a synonym for ignorance and also to signify the cosmic 'illusion' veiling the absolute Brahman.[13]

It is only in comparison with *Brahman* that it is unreal. In Samartha's words,

> Since Brahman alone is *advitiya*, one without a second, everything else must be regarded as *maya* in the sense of having no absolute reality but only a dependent or derived status. The ontological status of the world cannot be *sat* (Being), like that of the *Brahman*; neither can it be *asat* (non-being).[14]

There is in fact no great gulf between this and the statement of Deutero-Isaiah, taken up in the New Testament (I Peter 1.24f.), that

> All flesh is grass
> and all its beauty like the flower of the field. . . .
> The grass withers, the flower fades;
> but the word of our God will stand for ever (40.6,8).

The difference is that the 'flesh' for the biblical writers does not 'veil' or conceal God: it reveals him, and supremely so in the New Testament. Salvation is not to be found by turning one's back on matter. But for the Hindu-Buddhist tradition liberation (*moksha* or *mukti*) means freedom from attachment to this lesser reality, this screen of appearances. It involves the renunciation of worldly craving which draws us apart from the ground of our being, stripping away the five sheaths or *koshas* (of the physical, the vital, the mental, the intellectual and the spiritual) that obscure the *atman*, the real self,

---

[12] On this cf. Radhakrishnan, *Bhagavadgita*, pp. 37–43, and Samartha, *Introduction to Radhakrishnan*, pp. 57–63.

[13] *The Vedic Experience*, p. 883. For the history of this fundamental concept, see the major study by Devanandan, *The Concept of Maya*.

[14] *The Hindu Response*, p. 182. Equally the lower knowledge is not 'error'. It is 'ignorance' only when mistaken for the higher. Cf. Otto, interpreting Shankara, *Mysticism East and West*, pp. 153f.

and inhibit its union with reality. It is release from the round of desire and suffering, from the accumulated entail of cause and effect (*karma*), and ultimately from the cycle of re-becoming and the chain of rebirth. *Nirvana* is the cessation of *karma* and *samsara*, the 'snuffing out' of the individual conditioned ego and its false perspectives. In Hinduism this means the union of the self with the Absolute in what the *Gita* (2.72; 5.24) calls *brahma-nirvana*. In Buddhism it means the annihilation, not indeed of the self because, according to the doctrine of *anatta*, or no-self, there is no self to annihilate, but of the illusion of individual selfhood and of all that rekindles the flame of desire with its craving to exist and re-exist. In *nirvana* 'the fire has gone out because there is no longer any fuel to feed it'.[15] In both it is attained by the 'journey inwards', to use Dag Hammarskjold's phrase, the way of inner knowledge (*jnana*) and meditation (*dhyana*), of concentration, transcending and controlling not only the passions but the mind, seeking the goal of pure colourless light beyond the many-coloured dome of sense-experience and conceptual thinking. Its aim is enlightenment rather than transformation, involution rather than involvement, let alone revolution. The process has been described by a writer on Hindu mysticism as one of a steady disinclination towards worldly things and an indifference to worldly states.[16] The final union of *atman* and *Brahman*, of the soul with God, is pure spirit – *saccidananda*, being-consciousness-bliss, which is not only non-intellectual but non-intuitional, without reason or feeling. It is becoming impervious to grief, suffering and evil, rising above them rather than wrestling through them to a victory out the other side. The traditional image is that of the lotus leaf which the water may cover but can never make wet.[17] Thus even Abhishiktananda writes of

those Buddhist monks whose gentle, almost imperceptible smile,

---

[15] L. A. de Silva, *Buddhism: Beliefs and Practices in Sri Lanka*, p. 77; cf. also his valuable study, *The Problem of the Self in Buddhism and Christianity*, where he correlates the *anatta* doctrine with a relational view of man dependent on Buber's *I and Thou*.

[16] Dasgupta, *Hindu Mysticism*, p. 73.

[17] *Bhagavadgita* 5.10.

speaks of their distant compassion and their supreme indifference towards all that moves outside the circle of their inner retreat.[18]

From within the Indian tradition itself Hermann Hesse distinguishes, in the climax to his percipient novel *Siddhartha*, between the Buddhist ideal of invulnerability and the vulnerability of love to being touched and tied by relationships. And Suzuki epitomizes the difference between Buddhism and Christianity, and for him the manifest superiority of the former, by drawing attention to the fact that Gautama passed away prone and in peace, while Jesus died vertically and in agony.[19] Others desiring to soften the 'offence' of the gospel at this point have sought to present a 'yogic' Christ, unruffled even by crucifixion.[20]

The hallmark of this way of life is non-violence, or abstaining from hurt, *ahimsa*, and the renunciation of matter, power and machinery which formed such a central part of the message of Gandhi.[21] Its dominant ethos has been world-denying, anti-sexual, apolitical.

But the very mention of Gandhi, who with his firm belief in the transforming power of truth (*satyagraha*) was in his own distinctive way highly political and a profound social reformer, is reminder enough that this centre, especially when open as it was in his case to insights from elsewhere, is far from negative in its response to man and the world. This was argued most persuasively and attractively by Radhakrishnan in answer to Schweitzer[22] and to Heiler, who surely made a major error in saying that 'the fundamental psychic experience in mysticism is the denial of the impulse of life, a denial born of weariness of life'.[23] The supreme and most paradoxical instance of this outward turning to the world is the *boddhisattva* ideal in Mahayana Buddhism, of the saint who sacrifices

---

[18] *Saccidananda*, p. 148.

[19] *Mysticism, Christian and Buddhist*, pp. 137f.

[20] Cf. Parrinder, *Avatar and Incarnation*, pp. 231–3.

[21] Cf. the revealing quotations from Gandhi and the criticisms of him at this point by Tagore and Andrews, in Thomas, *The Acknowledged Christ*, pp. 218–25.

[22] Radhakrishnan, 'Mysticism and Ethics in Hindu Thought', in *Eastern Religions and Western Thought*, ch. 3, replying to A. Schweitzer, *Indian Thought and its Development*.

[23] *Prayer*, p. 142.

his own bliss for the sake of saving and serving others.[24] According to this ideal, if I really love myself, I must not love myself. Compassion for man still trapped in the toils of ignorance and unreality, if not love for man in changing the concrete particulars of poverty, disease and injustice, is a marked feature of Buddhism, and the self-immolation of the Vietnamese monks was a vivid act of *political* witness.[25] Moreover the work of the Ramakrishna Mission (the very name is significant) and of the Gandhi ashrams and the combination of worldliness and other-worldliness in men like Vinoba Bhave with his land-gift movement, not to mention the utopian vision of a city of God on earth to be built in Auroville,[26] is a sufficient indication that Hinduism sees the spiritual as positively related to the material, and today it has a strongly secular dimension.[27]

Moreover, the central issue of the *Gita* is concerned with action in the world – ironically 'the ruthless prosecution of a just but senseless war'[28] – yet without attachment to the fruits of action,[29] which Gandhi called 'the gospel of selfless action'. It even carries overtones of the Protestant work-ethic. As Bede Griffiths has observed,

> The Bhagavad Gita declared that the householder doing the ordinary duties of life could attain salvation no less than the

[24] For a sympathetic exposition of this ideal, cf. Bhikshu Sangharakshita, *The Three Jewels*, ch. 16 ('The Glorious Company of Bodhisattvas'). (He is an Englishman who became a Buddhist monk in India and was the author of the lecture I referred to earlier, 'Buddhism and the Bishop of Woolwich'.) He points out that in modern times liberal Mahayanists, especially in Japan, have begun to see this as a category for interpreting the spiritual masters of other religions, including Jesus (p. 202).

[25] One should also mention the movements within Buddhism to view its analysis of matter, as continuity without permanence, as in line with dynamic philosophies of process and creative evolution. See Thomas, *Man and the Universe of Faiths*, pp. 84f.

[26] A major project of the Aurobindo Ashram near Pondicherry. The reality, including relations with the neighbourhood and even with the Ashram itself, we found to be less impressive.

[27] Cf. Devanandan, *Christian Concern in Hinduism*, especially chs. 4 and 5; and R. Antoine and P. Fallon in *Religious Hinduism*, ch. 29.

[28] Zaehner, *Hinduism*, p. 97. There is no word of moral discernment, as in the prophetic tradition – just the reassurance that the eternal Spirit in man is in any case beyond destruction in war (2.17–25).

[29] 3.19; 18.1–63. Cf. Radhakrishnan, *Bhagavadgita*, pp. 66–75: 'The *Gita* advocates detachment from desires and not cessation from work' (p. 68).

ascetic in the forest. Man could be saved by work: all that was
required was that the work should be done with detachment. It
is work that is done with attachment, that is, with selfish motives
that binds the soul.[30]

Indeed K. M. Panikkar in his book *Foundations of the New
India* draws attention to the role that the *Gita* has played in
sanctioning action for change:

> It provided a new ethic: it enabled new social ideals to be for-
> mulated without apparently violating orthodoxy: it allowed the
> philosophy of Hindus, so long considered to be contemplative
> and world-denying, to be interpreted as a dynamic doctrine for
> action for the welfare of the world. In fact it gave to modern
> India a scripture, which, at once orthodox and universally
> accepted, was also, so to say, a handbook of revolution.[31]

Just as the *advaita* philosophy is adjusting to history, so
'the manner in which Vedanta is interpreted as a "social
Gospel"', as the spiritual basis of an ideology of secular
humanism, is perhaps the most radical transformation in
Hindu doctrine and life that has taken place through the
years'.[32] Vivekananda, giving to Ramakrishna's teaching a
twist that it never really had, set the trail, though neither he
nor the Ramakrishna Mission would appear to have worked
out a serious *theological* basis for their social service programme.[33] Radhakrishnan, the philosophical idealist, claims
that 'in my writings I have interpreted the doctrine of *maya*
so as to save the world and give it real meaning'[34] and make
possible 'a secularity that is spiritual'.[35] 'The opposite of outward action', he has insisted, with the *Gita*, 'is not inaction
but inward action'.[36] 'The distinctive feature of the Hindu
view is that it does not look upon the development of mind,
life, and body as the primary ends of life'[37] – not that it

---

[30] *Return to the Centre*, p. 140. Cf. especially 3.31; 4.23f., 41; 5.10; 6.1f.; 18.41–8.
[31] *Foundations of the New India*, p. 37; quoted, Thomas, *Man and the Universe
of Faiths*, pp. 63f.; cf. his whole chapter on the values and goals of the Hindu
renaissance, pp. 63–80.
[32] Thomas, op. cit., p. 64.
[33] Cf. Samartha, *The Hindu Response*, pp. 59f.
[34] *The Philosophy of Radhakrishnan*, ed. P. A. Schlipp, p. 800.
[35] Radhakrishnan, *Religion and Society*, p. 106.
[36] *Eastern Religions and Western Thought*, p. 107. Cf. *Bhagavadgita* 3.4–9.
[37] Op cit., p. 99.

denigrates them. On the contrary, he adduces the beautiful image of the *Maitri Upanishad* (1.2) where the knower of the self is compared to a smokeless fire burning with an inner glow, and comments: 'The body becomes a transparency through which the spirit shines, a glass for its indwelling flame'.[38]

There is also the remarkable verse from the *Taittirya Upanishad* (3.2),

> Food is *Brahman*: for from food creatures are born; by food the creatures thus born live; and into food they enter and perish,

on which Appasamy seized, together with Ramanuja's teaching that all created beings are 'the body of God', for interpreting the eucharist.[39] Moreover the traditional Hindu attitude to sex, and especially to the erotic in the Shaivite cults, has been a good deal more integrative (while at the same time strangely suppressive of touch and actual emotional relationships) than much that has passed for Christianity under Gnostic and Manichean influence. In *bhakti* too, as Bishop Stephen Neill emphasized in his Teape Lectures[40], the goal of desirelessness becomes engulfed in a passionate and spontaneous love of God as fervent and as rapturous as anything in Western love-mysticism.[41]

Aurobindo and Teilhard

Yet for all their points of convergence and overlap it is important to recognize that the two centres still view matter in subtly different ways. A comparison may perhaps best be made by bringing together two almost contemporary figures, Eastern and Western, who independently arrived at strikingly similar philosophies, Sri Aurobindo Ghose and Père Teilhard de Chardin. Both had a deeply spiritual panentheistic vision

---

[38] Op. cit., p. 98.

[39] *Christianity as Bhakti Marga*, p. 132, cf. pp. 142–77; and *The Gospel and India's Heritage*, pp. 206, 208; quoted Boyd, *Indian Christian Theology*, pp. 138–40.

[40] S. C. Neill, *Bhakti Hindu and Christian*.

[41] Cf. Dasgupta, *Hindu Mysticism*, chs. 5 and 6; O'Flaherty, *Asceticism and Eroticism in the Mythology of Siva*; and Dhavamony, *Love of God according to the Saiva Siddhanta*.

of the evolutionary process which yet took matter very seriously. Each was, as it were, on the near wing of his own camp.

Aurobindo had an exceptionally strong feel for the body as divine and like St Paul, saw the destiny of man in a kind of *soma pneumatikon* or spiritual body, except that he *did* think that flesh and blood could possess it (contrast I Cor. 15.50) and envisaged the imminent arrival of some form of 'super-nature' and state of physical immortality. Moreover he made a real attempt to incorporate the insights of evolutionary theory into a Hindu world-view and his Integral Yoga sought to bring everything physical, mental and supra-mental, into a whole which includes every aspect of cultural and corporate living. It is a massive and inspiring synthesis.[42]

Teilhard too combined being a 'scientist' and a 'seer', to use the terms of Charles Raven, the first lecturer in the Teape series. Teilhard spent many of the best years of his life in China and was fascinated by the vision of integrating what he called 'the road of the East' and 'the road of the West' – though whether he really understood the East any more profoundly than Aurobindo the West must remain doubtful.[43] Yet for all his roots in the biblical, and especially the Pauline tradition, Teilhard's sympathies were not instinctively for the 'Thou', for the neighbour. Even in his 'personalizing' mysticism – for there is no doubt that his goal is communion, not absorption – there is a frank confession that 'other people' are more like hell than heaven:

> I find no difficulty in integrating into my inward life everything above and beneath me ... in the universe – whether matter, plants, animals; and then powers, dominions and angels: these I can accept without difficulty. . . . But 'the other man', my God – by which I do not mean 'the poor, the halt, the lame and the sick', but 'the other' quite simply as 'other', the one who seems

---

[42] For a sympathetic Western Christian introduction see the number of the American Roman Catholic journal *Cross Currents*, 22.1, Winter 1972, entirely devoted to his life, thought and legacy. For an Indian Christian assessment cf. J. A. Chakalamattam in *Unique and Universal*, ed. J. B. Chethimattam, pp. 125–31.

[43] See Ursula M. King, *Towards a New Mysticism: Teilhard de Chardin and Eastern Religions*; and Zaehner's Teape Lectures, *Evolution in Religion*, pp. 17f.

to exist independently of me because his universe seems closed to mine, and who seems to shatter the unity and the silence of the world for me – would I be sincere if I did not confess that my instinctive reaction is to rebuff him? and that the mere thought of entering into spiritual communication with him disgusts me?[44]

That indeed was an early reaction.[45] Later in an essay written in Peking in 1942 called 'The Rise of the Other' he recognized, to quote its closing words, that

the irresistible rise of the other all around us, and its intrusion even into our individual lives, is without any possible doubt the expression and measure of our own ascent into the personal.[46]

Yet these two seemingly sympathetic souls reveal an attitude to matter which is interestingly different. One of Teilhard's last writings, composed in 1950, was called *La Coeur de la Matière*, but the *double entendre* is inevitably lost in the English title *The Heart of Matter*.[47] He believed passionately in matter, '*la sainte matière*',[48] as 'the matrix of spirit'.[49] He wrote a hymn to it,[50] and his 'Mass on the World'[51] is a profound meditation on the entire material order as a sacrament of the divine: 'I firmly believe that everything around me is the body and blood of the Word.'[52] In contrast with what he saw as the Hindu view of matter as 'dead weight and illusion' he viewed it as 'heavily loaded, throughout, with sublime possibilities'.[53] He shocked his religious order by such statements as this:

If as a result of some interior revolution, I were successively to

[44] *Le Milieu Divin*, p. 138.
[45] For the painful transition, cf. *Writings in Time of War*, pp. 30f.
[46] *The Activation of Energy*, p. 75. I owe this reference and much else at this point to conversation and correspondence with Dr King.
[47] But he did refer in a letter to 'the Graham Greene title (*The Heart of the Matter*)', which he said 'would be wonderful for me (although with quite a different meaning)', op. cit., p. 77.
[48] In a letter of 18 August 1950, quoted, op. cit., p. 77.
[49] Ibid., p. 35.
[50] *Hymn of the Universe*, pp. 68–71.
[51] Ibid., pp. 17–37; the final version is reprinted in *The Heart of Matter*, pp. 119–34.
[52] *Hymn of the Universe*, p. 28; *The Heart of Matter*, p. 127.
[53] *Christianity and Evolution*, p. 122.

lose my faith in Christ, my faith in a personal God, my faith in the Spirit, I think I would still continue to believe in the World. The World (the value, the infallibility, the goodness of the World): that, in the final analysis, is the first and last thing in which I believe.[54]

That is *not* the credo of a pure cosmic pantheist. But it does indicate his point of attachment and departure. He was a post-secular scientific man, and he was a scientist before he was a seer – though many scientists have accused him of seriously confounding the categories in *his* 'integral yoga'. But no one can dispute that he was a professional palaeontologist with a deeply grounded training in the exact sciences and a strong commitment to the inductive method. This was for him the way *into* truth, however much it might run *out* into mystery.

In Aurobindo there is little or nothing of this. He does not have one foot, or even one toe, in the laboratory and there is no attempt to wrestle with the empirical evidence either in the natural or the human sciences.[55] His way in is purely intuitive. For him spirit is the heart of the matter, rather than *vice versa*. Spirit is indeed in the process of manifesting itself, realizing itself, through matter, but by leaving it behind and returning in upon itself. He speaks of the 'self-unfolding' of spirit, of the evolution of what has previously been involuted. It is still indeed a world-affirming and world-transforming approach. Matter is in no way illusory or unholy. It is creative energy (*shakti*), play (*lila*), joy (*ananda*) – part of the exuberant delight of existence. Yet as one of his interpreters has put it, 'for "a divine life upon earth" spirit and matter are equally essential but not equally divine'.[56] Matter is the lowest

[54] *How I Believe*, quoted by H. de Lubac, *The Faith of Teilhard de Chardin*, p. 136, who has to devote the whole of the second half of his book to defending this passage. *Le Milieu Divin* is dedicated to 'those who love the world'.

[55] Zaehner makes the same point: 'On the whole Aurobindo mistrusted science and particularly medical science, for which he had an irrational and obscurantist aversion. His tribute to it, such as it is, seems to be only lip-service paid to a fashionable idol. In this he differs widely from Teilhard for whom scientific research was akin to adoration and who could say: "Neither in its impetus nor in its achievements can science go to its limits without becoming tinged with mysticism and charged with faith" ', *Evolution in Religion*, p. 37.

[56] McDermott in *Six Pillars*, p. 171.

and least valuable form of life, destined to be transcended by a ladder of ascent, reminiscent of the Gnostics and Neoplatonists, through the spheres of mind and super-mind. In fact he does not hesitate to speak of the evolution of 'a supramental or gnostic race of beings', and says that the gnostic being will be alone with God, self-plunged into the depth of the Infinite. Nothing will be able to disturb him or invade the depths or bring him down from the summit – yet the peace of God within him will be extended in a universal calm of equality not merely passive but dynamic.[57] And this is reflected in his description of the attitude to matter of 'the spiritual man' (to borrow the phrase St Paul took over from the Corinthian Gnostics):

> There will be in him a certain respect for physical things, an awareness of the occult consciousness in them.

For

> the gnostic light and power can unite with Matter, so seen, and accept it as an instrument of a spiritual manifestation. A certain reverence even for Matter and a sacramental attitude in all dealings with it is possible.[58]

The reluctance and the reservations even in this positive acceptance are, I think, revealing of the difference of consciousness.

The Western and Eastern diseases

I have been comparing and contrasting two kindred spirits. But of course for the most part the gulf is a good deal greater and it is worth looking once more at the distortions that take over when either approach is pressed in isolation from the other.

It scarcely needs spelling out that the 'Western disease' – all too contagious in the second and third worlds – is materialism, making an 'ism' out of matter. It represents the reign of

[57] Summarizing in his own words from *The Future Evolution of Man: The Life Divine Upon Earth*, an anthology of his writings by P. B. Saint-Hilaire, pp. 114f.
[58] Quoted from *The Life Divine*, in *The Future Evolution of Man*, pp. 118f.

the outward over the inward, of the masculine over the feminine, the *yang* over the *yin*. It manifests itself in the creeping evils of bureaucracy and technocracy, urbanization and centralization, in the diseases of stress and pollution, the crushing inequalities of wealth and power, not to mention the final prostitution of matter in the nuclear bomb. It exalts the demonic mystery of money over the divine mystery of bread. E. F. Schumacher found it necessary to give to his manifesto *Small is Beautiful* the ironic sub-title 'Economics as if people mattered'. For it seems to growing numbers to produce a way of life that is destructive of persons and spiritually sterile. It has led too to an over-emphasis on intellectualization, to an imbalance of thought over feeling, with suppression and loss once again of the intuitive and feminine. There have indeed been prophets of protest in the West, from Jung to Alan Watts and Laurence van der Post, from Rosenstock-Huessy to Ivan Illich and Schumacher, who have been heard gladly – and largely ignored. Yet by now there is a groundswell of reaction especially among the young and the middle-classes in favour of a more 'Eastern' and holistic life-style, with emphasis on devolution, conservation, 'soft' energy programmes, the 'green' revolution and 'appropriate' technology. It is *not* anti-material or anti-scientific or anti-mechanical, but it witnesses with active non-violence against erecting any of these agencies into a juggernaut – a word imported, ironically, from India. It comes from a title of Krishna, *Jagannath*, 'Lord of the world' – and hence his idol on an enormous car, such as we saw near Serampore, under which his devotees are supposed to have thrown themselves. So the traffic is not simply one-way!

But from the other side there are to be seen, as it looks to many in the West, effects of the disavowal of matter closely parallel to those of the depreciation of history. It appears to result in a way of life, parodied by the yogi on his bed of nails, which bespeaks an acute denial of the body as the enemy of spirit. It issues in a benign, and often a malign, neglect; tolerating the intolerable in the way of suffering and disease, poverty and dirt, leaving men and women to die loveless and alone. Indifferentism, stagnation, fatalism, resignation to the rigidities of caste, an approach to matter symbolized by 'untouchability' – all these are symptoms just as destructive of the personal as those of materialism. And even at its best the ideal of selflessness (the renunciation of *jivatva*) is by no means obviously identical with unselfishness (the renunciation of *ahamkara*). In fact the concentration on the self and on the individual's release can seemingly lead to a higher selfishness which is not always so evidently spiritual. Cultivation of the 'gnostic' life is not the most obvious basis for being one's brother's keeper. Even in the *Gita* beloved of Gandhi the ideal is self-harmony rather than neighbour-love. In fact it has been observed that while in Hinduism the individual is firmly subordinated to the family, the caste and the sub-caste, Hinduism is also the most individualistic and least other-regarding of all the great religions. It makes for communalism, or sectional selfishness, the bane of Indian politics (and even of the Indian church[59]), rather than for community.

Buddhism too tends towards a placid suffering by identification rather than a will to transform the social structures. As Tillich puts it with great condensation, 'participation leads to agape, identity to compassion';[60] and the one has a revolutionary, the other a profoundly conservative thrust. Contrasting the 'hot' God of the covenant with the 'cool' approach of the Buddhist *arahant*, Kosuke Koyama writes:

> His direction is not *away from* history (detachment – 'eyes lowered'), but *towards* history (attachment – 'I have seen the affliction of my people who are in Egypt'). Perhaps this is the basic contrast between Theravada Buddhism and the Judaeo-Christian faith: the two histories, the two eyes.[61]

The renunciation of matter is in constant danger of becom-

---

[59] Cf. the searing remarks of Newbigin to his fellow Indian Christians on the church as a 'communal organization' in *The Good Shepherd: Meditations on Christian Ministry in Today's World*, pp. 169–73; and Thomas, *Salvation and Humanisation*, p. 60, on the form of the church as 'one self-regarding religious community among many such religious communities'. For the alternative of 'secular solidarity with all men', cf. Thomas, *Man and the Universe of Faiths*, ch. 6; and Choan-Seng Song, *Christian Mission in Reconstruction – An Asian Attempt*.

[60] *Christianity and the Encounter of the World Religions*, p. 70.

[61] *Waterbuffalo Theology*, pp. 152f.

ing the renunciation of society and of the responsibility for power on which justice is based. I remember talking with one of my own students with strongly Buddhist inclinations, who has since taken an outstanding first in religious studies – and then given them up – who first came up to Cambridge at the time of a by-election. I asked him as a conversational gambit how he was going to vote. 'I am not going to vote.' When I looked quizzical he added, 'I am never going to vote.' It turned out that he had a completely quietist attitude to politics and the striving for power – clearly thought out and in its own way very searching. But it has left me pondering ever since.[62] Is responsibility for democracy to be left then to the rest of us? That is an attitude on which Hitler would have thrived.

In fact there goes with all this a certain authoritarianism which comes through in the various spiritual movements and their gurus that hit us, with increasingly rapid turnover, in the West. They presuppose a one-sided master-pupil relationship, epitomized in the spiritual autocracy of the Mother in the Aurobindo experiment, now left rudderless and divided. Some of these movements have brought real liberation and 'soul'. But others are frankly financial rackets or dangerously like brain-washing. And when even the Maharishi and his Transcendental Meditation[63] get yoked to the technology of transatlantic media and money I fear whether the last state may not be worse than the first. As Harvey Cox puts it in his entertaining but perceptive book *Turning East: The Promise and the Peril of the New Orientalism,*

> Alfred Loisy once remarked that Jesus came preaching the Kingdom of God but what happened was the church. It could be said similarly of many of the current Eastern masters that they came teaching enlightenment but what happened was yet another spate of American self-improvement sects (p. 136).

But these are the excesses, largely for export only. There is

[62] Cf. also the question Tillich raises as to whether Buddhism, with no doctrine of individuality, and therefore of inalienable and equal rights, can provide a spiritual foundation for democracy in Japan, op. cit., pp. 74f.

[63] For an independent but sympathetic assessment of this movement, cf. Una Kroll, *TM: A Signpost for the World.*

much genuine spiritual commerce. Krishnamurti and yoga, for instance, have helped thousands. And if the world had begun to despair of democracy in the East (as there are plenty who despair of it also in the West), it recently had a sharp reminder of the life still left in the electoral processes both of India and Sri Lanka – though whether, from its sheer scale, the former in particular is governable is a question which the visitor is left uneasily wondering.

The transfiguration of matter

Yet where, once more, between these distortions, is wholeness to be found? At this point above all there must surely be a complementarity which does justice to each pole. Both attitudes to matter must be held together in their strengths and mutual tensions, rather than in compromise or dilution, if a healthy balance is to be achieved for the individual and the world.

I observed earlier how that book *The Tao of Physics* by Fritjof Capra, himself a product of Europe and now of the American West, noted the striking coincidences between modern particle physics and Eastern religious thought-forms. There is a growing sensitivity that the presuppositions of Western (in contrast, say, with Chinese) science have yielded a falsified picture of the universe, and that we must get back, or move forward, to more holistic and 'fieldish' ways of thinking. What he did not perhaps sufficiently acknowledge was that this new awareness is coming to the fore (and that largely by advances in quantum physics pioneered by the West) as a corrective to a monumental enterprise which would never have got off the ground at all, at any rate when it did and as it did, without the insights of Western spirituality, and especially of the biblical doctrines of creation and man. Science and technology could not have made much progress unless they had been able to assume the validity of the more dualistic stance, which enables the subject for the purposes of the experiment to stand back in relative isolation and abstract himself as 'I' to 'It' from the object under observation. While the *limitations* of Newtonian physics may have owed much to the distortions of Cartesian dual*ism*, with its isolation of the *res extensa* of matter from the *res cogitans* of mind, its fantastic achievements would equally have been impossible without many of its presuppositions. Moreover the findings of this approach still hold good of the macrocosmic realm of everyday experienced reality, however much their validity may need to be qualified at the sub-atomic level. It is surely clear that neither perspective can represent the whole truth in isolation: the 'outside' and 'inside' of things cannot be separated. But the corollary of that must be that the spirituality which has contributed so signally to the understanding of the one and the spirituality that comports so fascinatingly with the other cannot also be held apart, nor the one merely reduced to the other. Each requires and needs its polar opposite.

I pleaded in the book of mine I mentioned earlier, *Exploration into God* – and the preposition in the title indicates the direction of the spirituality – for what I called paradoxically a 'secular mysticism'. This means taking with equal and apparently opposite seriousness two of the more significant movements, as I read them, in theological and philosophical thinking today. The one recognizes, as Dietrich Bonhoeffer stressed in his last *Letters and Papers from Prison* before dying at the hands of the Nazis, that there is no return now to a pre-secular, pre-scientific, 'sacral' culture. There has been an irreversible movement of the human spirit, reaching back in the West four hundred years, on which the East too is rapidly catching up. This process of secularization Bonhoeffer interpreted positively as God teaching man to grow up, to be independent or, better, interdependent. It is an insight which itself stems from the prophetic tradition, with its de-sacralizing strain[64], culminating in the 'death' of God as understood in the relationship of 'religious' dependence. It says to man, like Yahweh to Ezekiel: 'Son of man, stand upon thy feet, and I will speak with thee' (Ezek. 2.1). It affirms the relationship, the frightening relationship, not merely of responsibility to but of responsibility for – the world, history, matter. And in our generation that responsibility has come to

[64] Cf. Harvey Cox, *The Secular City*, ch. 1.

seem almost one of being 'as gods, knowing good and evil'.
That was indeed the promise held out by the serpent in the
myth of the Garden of Eden (Gen. 3.5). But the true relationship is what the New Testament calls that of being not
'gods' but 'sons'. This does not mean an attitude of puerile
dependence – sons in our imagination never seem to grow up
– but precisely of maturity, of 'man come of age', in contrast
both with children and slaves (cf. especially Gal. 4.1–7). It is
a relationship of freedom in responsibility. It accepts man in
what Bonhoeffer called his 'worldliness', which is very different from living *for* the world and its values. It does not require
him to put the clock back on his science and technology, his
secularity or even his modern sexuality. (One gets the impression, no doubt unfairly, from Bede Griffiths' otherwise impressive *Return to the Centre* that almost everything that has
happened since the Renaissance, not to mention the Reformation, has been a mistake!) For all these can be paths to
freedom – from the paternalistic society, through the follies
and casualties of the permissive society, to the mature society.

And there is a great deal more liberation to be won than
the West in its complacency has yet recognized. What the
Latin Americans have taught us to call by the ugly word
'conscientization', the stirring to awareness of personal, historical and material freedom, is an essential part of becoming
a child of God and an inheritor of the kingdom of heaven.
Yet these are dangerous awakenings, as church and state,
right and left, have always found. And they must find expression in structures, in politics, in freedom-movements and
power-struggles. For power, as atomic power vividly reminds
us, is only a function of matter. That does not necessarily
mean violence. Indeed, as President Kennedy said, in words
that constantly came to mind in South Africa and Israel, it
is 'those who make the peaceful revolution impossible who
make the violent revolution inevitable'. Yet no view of man,
no religion, no theology that does not take these things
seriously today has itself the right to be taken seriously. Matter matters.

That is one side, the side that begins from the outside and
works from there *into* God, the Christ and the self with an

ultimate, and not merely a proximate, concern for persons, for history, for matter. But equally, and apparently oppositely, there is another side, which seeks first the 'return to the centre' and to work from there outwards. And who shall dare to say they are incompatible or that, as Kipling supposed of East and West, never the twain shall meet?

This second approach starts by affirming that 'the one thing necessary', the pearl of great price, is at all costs to touch reality, to find the one beyond and within the many, the centred self beneath all the layers which the ego constructs. For this approach the material world is *not* as such illusory or sinful, but it is a distraction and can become a delusion. Prior con-centration or simplification (as the Neoplatonists long ago called it) or even, with the Buddhists, emptiness and annihilation, is the only route to freedom *from*, which is a prerequisite of freedom *for*. Detachment is a *sine qua non*.

But there are two kinds of detachment. They are distinguished in the book I quoted earlier by Charles Davis, the Roman Catholic theologian who himself 'came out' from a fairly secluded and negative ecclesiastical upbringing:

> The first is to take it as the eradication or deadening of all affectivity, especially sensuous. The second is to see it as the retrieval of the self-transcending, self-forgetting dynamism of all human, sensuous affectivity when no longer dominated by the ego.[65]

He wishes to differentiate sharply between sensuousness and sensuality, and his whole book, full of suggestive insights, is a plea for the recovery of 'feeling' in religion, or in the words of its deliberately paradoxical title, for body *as* spirit. In the paraphrase of the dust-cover summary,

> Sensuousness is the act of participating in the spontaneous rhythms and responses of the body with its joys and delights as well as its pain and stress. It implies in fact a sacramental, mystical view of the world. Far from being an enslaving subjection of the mind to bodily impulses, like sensuality, sensuousness is a total response to reality coming from the unity of the self as an embodied person.

[65] *Body as Spirit*, p. 58.

He speaks of the 'asceticism of achieved spontaneity', and this is very close to the Zen ideal, the liberation of being free to do what comes naturally, of *wu-wei*, or non-action, which is yet as positive and spontaneous as the grass growing.[66]

Nevertheless, unlike some salesmen of instant mysticism, he refuses any suggestion that technique can hold the key. He says:

> Those who, like myself, do not believe that a first innocence is available, and who insist that we must all be born again, cannot suppose that techniques of sensory awareness – yoga, Zen methods of concentration and of artless art, and so on – will of themselves suffice . . . . The new asceticism, like the old, is meaningless unless it carries with it a transformation of conscious life, repentance and conversion.

And he concludes with the striking statement that 'if people would stop maltreating their bodies as machines for their egocentric purposes, they might be drawn to take the first steps in the mystical ascent'.[67]

That of course is as much a judgment upon Western lifestyles as on Eastern. And it is important to recognize that there is also a false marriage of East and West, which, so far from leading to a transformation of the whole person and the world, results in a 'throw-away' attitude to both, or what Harvey Cox calls 'consumer detachment'.

> Our American form of detachment comes not from the spiritual insight that all things are moving towards nothingness, but from planned obsolescence, from fashion changes and the constant introduction of new products to replace the ones we love. Our form of 'detachment' is a kind of alienation that also infects relationships to persons, not just things.

And he explains how one may get the worst and not the best of both visions of reality:

> Western religion tends to accept the ego but teaches that love as a positive form of attachment can replace possessiveness and manipulation. Eastern spirituality does not give love such a cen-

---

[66] Cf. Watts, *The Way of Zen*, part 2, ch. 2.
[67] *Body as Spirit*, p. 57.

tral place, but teaches that ego is unreal, and that all forms of attachment lead to suffering. The prism-distorted Western version of Buddhism combines the loveless ego with psychological 'detachment'. What comes out looks much like irresponsibility with a spiritual cover, a metaphysical licence to avoid risky, demanding relationships, a mystical permit to skip from one person, bed, cause or program without ever taking the plunge.[68]

The only kind of mysticism for which a truly two-eyed vision of man and the material would wish to contend is one that takes the 'diaphany of the divine at the heart of a glowing universe',[69] the transfiguration both of persons and of things, more seriously rather than less. This is a mysticism of love, yes, of justice.[70] It is concerned with what the New Testament calls 'the mystery of the kingdom of God' and the seeking first of his righteousness. Since about the only text that the popularizers of mysticism ever quote about the kingdom of God is that usually translated 'the kingdom of God is within you' (Luke 17.21) and since this is then interpreted in a purely internal, individual, gnosticizing manner, it is perhaps worth interjecting a word about it. In the first place the 'you' is plural. Secondly it is addressed to the opponents of Jesus. Thirdly, in context, it is a dissuasive against calculating the moment of God's in-breaking into history by looking for portents. It seems to mean either that, if you had the eyes to see it, the kingdom is already among you, at work in your midst in the words and works of the Messiah, or that it will suddenly be upon you, catching you unawares. In any case it concerns the redemption of history, the total transformation of this world-order, the victory of the divine mystery over the demonic. And that, for the whole New Testament, is won at the last only through the blood, sweat and tears of the final plumbing of matter to the depths which is crucifixion.

By way of contrast Vivekananda, citing the two gospel texts most commonly torn from their context, 'The kingdom of heaven is within you' and 'I and my Father are one' (which

[68] *Turning East*, pp. 137f.

[69] Teilhard de Chardin, *The Heart of Matter*, p. 16. Cf. King, 'Teilhard's Fundamental Vision', *The Ampleforth Journal* 83.3, 1978, pp. 11–21.

[70] Cf. Berdyaev, *Spirit and Reality*, ch. 6 ('Mysticism: its Contradictions and Achievements'), who also wants to affirm a 'prophetic mysticism'.

last in its setting of John 10.25–38 clearly refers to moral
unity rather than metaphysical identity[71]) presents Jesus as
'a disembodied, unfettered, unbound spirit' who realized himself as God in the core of his spirit and led others to the same
self-awareness.[72] It is in this way that he 'takes away the sin
of the world' – by showing us 'that we too are God':[73] 'It is
only necessary to clear away the dust and dirt, and then the
spirit shines immediately.'[74] As he put it elsewhere, 'Vedanta
recognizes no sin, it only recognizes error.'[75]

I suppose that no one from the 'prophetic' side ever really
thinks that the Hindu or Buddhist fully feels the weight of
moral evil.[76] Even Arjuna's cry for mercy in response to the
vision of Krishna at the climax of the *Gita* (11.40–45), which
is the nearest parallel to Isa. 6.1–7, is expressed in terms of
awe rather than of moral worthlessness. There is in these
great religions an acute sense of ignorance (*avidya*), which it
has been rightly said is not the opposite of knowledge but of
insight, of suffering (*duhkha*,[77] literally, as Panikkar reminds

---

[71] See ch. 5 below. Referring to the abuse of this text in Hinduism, Appasamy
says: 'This utterance has appealed to the religious heart of India, which because of
the monistic point of view so largely familiar to it, has defied all reasonable laws of
exegesis and has interpreted the passage to mean that Jesus, always one with God,
realized in a luminous moment this supreme identity. But we must remember that
Jesus always lived in a whole-hearted trust and faith in the Father. He did not
consider himself identical with God' (*What is Moksha? A Study in the Johannine
Doctrine of Life,* p. 2.) He later said that 'the *Mahavakya* of the Christian religion'
(corresponding to the 'Great Utterances' of the Upanishads about the unity of *atman*
and *Brahman*) is not 'I and my Father are one' but 'Abide in me and I in you', *My
Theological Quest,* p. 28. For his thought see Boyd, *Indian Christian Theology,*
pp. 118–43; and Thomas, *The Acknowledged Christ,* pp. 138–43.

[72] *Works* IV, pp. 145f.

[73] *Works* VII, p. 4.

[74] *Works* IV, p. 149. Cf. the very similar assessment of evil as dirt on the windows
or rust on the sword in the Japanese Buddhist tradition; Benedict, *Chrysanthemum
and Sword,* pp. 191f.

[75] Quoted by Samartha, *Introduction to Radhakrishnan,* p. 91.

[76] Cf. Neill, *Bhakti Hindu and Christian,* pp. 79f.

[77] This is of course one of the basic categories of Buddhism. It is very inadequately
rendered 'suffering'. The Dalai Lama (His Holiness Tenzin Gyatsho), to whom I
am much indebted for the copy of his book *The Opening of the Wisdom Eye,* opts
for 'unsatisfactoriness' (cf. the Greek *mataiotes,* 'vanity') and divides it, with the
Buddhist tradition, into 'the suffering of unsatisfactoriness,' 'the suffering of deterio-
ration' and 'the suffering of conformations'. 'The first means bodily and mental pain
which is actually felt and which cannot be other than unsatisfactory. The second is
the oppressive nature of all conditioned things which are bound to change and
deteriorate, while the third means the unsatisfactory nature of all that is formed or

us,[78] 'with a bad axle hole', and hence dis-stress), of *karma*, the external entail and pile-up of 'bad actions', but not to anything like the same degree[79] of sin.[80] And the same applies to the whole Gnostic tradition, which works with a meta-physical dualism between spirit and matter rather than a moral dualism between good and evil, and also to that strong strain within Western Catholicism which sees evil in terms of non-being or defect, as *deprivatio* rather than *depravatio*.

We have noted how a docetic, 'yogic' view of the cross has characterized the more mystical and Gnostic world-views from the beginning. So sympathetic an interpreter of Buddh-ism to the West as Suzuki, in the revealing essay from which I cited earlier on 'Crucifixion and Enlightenment',[81] contrasts the serenity of the Buddha even in death with the 'terrible sight' of the crucified Christ, which he says he 'cannot help associating . . . with the sadistic impulse of a physically affected brain'. And Aelred Graham in his 'Promptings from India'[82] notes the same reaction of a Buddhist monk to a crucifix: 'it caused him distress and he thought it a very repellent religious emblem'; and he adds in a footnote:

> This sentiment was expressed to me several times when I was in the East. The depiction of an almost naked human being nailed to a cross as an object to be revered is unintelligible, with its presentation of barbarous cruelty, to a devout Buddhist, who is disposed to regard violent death in any form as the result of 'bad karma'.[83]

St Paul, it has been well said, who also had to struggle with the 'curse of the law' attaching to anyone hanging on a tree

conditioned because of the dependent and precarious mode of its existence' (pp. 105f.).
[78] *The Vedic Experience*, p. 876.
[79] Though cf. the moving confession of the seventeenth-century Gujarati poet Dadudayal quoted by Boyd, *Indian Christian Theology*, p. 131, from Appasamy's valuable anthology, *Temple Bells*, p. 62.
[80] Cf. the observation of P. Younger, *Introduction to Indian Religious Thought*, p. 92: 'In the Indian account alienation because of sin and guilt were not the problem. Therefore the kind of polar relationship that is described by Martin Buber as an I-Thou relationship has very little appeal.'
[81] *Mysticism, Christian and Buddhist*, ch. 6.
[82] *The End of Religion: Autobiographical Explorations*, ch. 6.
[83] Ibid., p. 164.

(Gal. 3.13), never forgets that Jesus did not die a gentle death like Socrates. And contemplating the massive tranquillity of the Buddha statues at Gal Vihara, Polonnaruwa in Ceylon, one could feel the contrast, brilliantly caught in Thomas Merton's *Asian Journal*:

> The silence of the extraordinary faces. The great smiles. Huge and yet subtle. Filled with every possibility, questioning nothing, knowing everything, rejecting nothing, the peace not of emotional resignation but of . . . sunyata (emptiness), that has seen through every question without trying to discredit anyone or anything – *without refutation* – without establishing some other argument.[84]

'This', goes on Suzuki, 'is where Buddhism differs from Christianity.'

> Buddhism declares that there is from the beginning no self to crucify. To think that there is the self is the start of all errors and evils. Ignorance is at the root of all things that go wrong. . . . As there is no self, no crucifixion is needed, no sadism is to be practised, no shocking sight is to be displayed by the roadside.[85]

The Christian would want to reply that the sadism is in the world itself, and to say that 'no crucifixion is needed' is to blind oneself to the fact that there were, and have since been, countless crosses set up by man's inhumanity to man before ever Jesus took his place between two others. Rather, what Calvary shows is God, through a completely real man of flesh and blood entering right into the depth of that evil and refusing to burke it. And that is the price of resurrection and of the transfiguration of this entire very material body of history. This I believe is the *real* difference betwen Buddhism and Christianity.[86]

But I want to end not by stressing what are genuine and irreducible differences but by coming back to where I began, with the dialogue or 'speaking across' between the two centres. Inevitably I have been speaking primarily from where

[84] Op. cit., p. 233. I owe this reference to Bishop Lakshman Wickremesinghe of Kurunagala, with whom we were staying when visiting the statues.

[85] *Mysticism, Christian and Buddhist*, pp. 136f.

[86] Koyama makes the same point by contrasting the open hand of the Buddha and the closed fist of Lenin with the pierced hands of Jesus 'painfully neither open nor closed', *No Handle on the Cross*, pp. 22–7.

I am, and, equally inevitably, there has been more of me that
is identified with one pole than the other. That will be true
of everyone who shares internally the tension of which I have
been treating. I do not believe that we advance the dialogue
by toning down the tension: in fact at several points I have
deliberately sharpened it, though not, I hope, in such a way
as to be disputatious. But I would agree with those who
would remind us of the unavoidability of decision somewhere
along the line. Thus Newbigin writes out of his long experience of India of the same distinction between the mystical
and the prophetic view-points, while ranging himself fairly
squarely with the second:

> The Hindu mystic begins by abstracting himself from all appre-
> hensions of phenomena. It is therefore only to be expected that
> he ends with a state of pure unitary awareness, undisturbed by
> any kind of multiplicity. He has what he set out to seek. From
> the standpoint he has taken, all multiplicity has ceased to exist,
> because he has deliberately shut it out of his attention. But to
> conclude that this experience is the clue to ultimate reality is not
> a logical deduction, but a leap of faith; for the whole question is:
> What is the relation of that ultimate reality to the multiplicity of
> phenomena? We face here, surely, an ultimate decision, which
> is, in the last resort, a decision of faith; whether we regard the
> multiplicity and change which characterizes human life as a mere
> veil which has to be torn away in order that we may have access
> to ultimate reality, or whether we regard them as the place where
> we are to meet with and know and serve the divine purpose.[87]

Similarly, Charles Davis speaks of 'the debate . . . between
two world views, one for which relationships are of ultimate
significance and one for which they are not'.[88] As will have
become clear, if I had to opt, I would be with the former.
But I am not persuaded that the choice is between such a
simple disjunction. Faced with a dichotomy which rests on
such fundamental and *deeply spiritual* apprehensions of reality, I believe we must begin by attending to the 'both-and'
before we close too easily with an 'either-or'.

In a collection of essays now of a previous generation, P.

---

[87] *A Faith for this One World?* 1961, p. 39 (1965, p. 41); quoted in part by
Thomas, *The Acknowledged Christ*, p. 180.

[88] *Body as Spirit*, p. 85; cf. his earlier *Christ and the World Religions*, p. 34.

T. Raju explicitly contrasted the 'I and Thou' with the 'I and That', noting that the latter requires to be complemented by the former:

> Here I feel Indian philosophy is left undeveloped, and here is scope for further development. It is not a mere speculative consideration, but a consideration for a philosophy of life. The mere neutral That, unless it develops into a personal Thou, cannot offer itself as an object for moral activity.[89]

He is, I believe, too self-critical in confining this limitation to Indian philosophy, though the first step for each of us must be humbly to hear what the other emphasis has to say to us. But he is right in recognizing that the distinction he alludes to is 'not a mere speculative consideration'. The line of which I have been speaking cuts through each one of us and touches life at so many points, spiritual and personal, social and political, that it is vital that we should grow together in the practical and not merely the theoretical recognition that in this and many other aspects 'truth is two-eyed'. We may not, through lack of practice, see very well through the eye we have not been accustomed to using. But in the process we are impoverished, truth suffers, and the world is neglected.

---

[89] *Contemporary Indian Philosophy*, ed. Radhakrishnan and Muirhead, [2]1952, p. 533.

CHAPTER V

The Uniqueness of Christ

Uniqueness and universality

Till now we have been looking at the validity of two 'eyes' on reality and arguing for their complementarity without reference to the specific truth-claim of any one religion. Nevertheless these distinctive truth-claims remain, and one of them is that which has lain at the very heart of Christianity, of the uniqueness and finality of Jesus as the Christ. Indeed it confronts an equal and opposite unspoken dogma in Hinduism of the non-uniqueness and non-finality of any *avatar* figure.[1] The purpose of dialogue again is not to eliminate or erode these two centres nor to suggest that there is ultimately no difference between them. But it is worth asking whether the conviction that truth is (at least) two-eyed may not only soften the edges – for acrimony (sharpness) and intransigence (the refusal to 'cross over') never achieved anything – but actually give new depth and illumination to the assertion that distinguishes Christianity from the other great faiths.

I deliberately begin this way, because the traditional approach has been to see other truth-claims and other eyes on reality to be a challenge and a threat, rather than a source of depth and illumination to the Christian view. In other words, the distinctiveness of the latter has, consciously or unconsciously, been identified with a one-eyed approach.

[1] This was stressed as a matter of principle by Vivekananda and Radhakrishnan. Cf. the discussion of the latter's thought at this point by Samartha, *The Hindu Response*, pp. 107–15, and the references given there.

That is why it was necessary earlier to labour the point that the difference between the two 'eyes' was *not* the difference between Christianity on the one hand and Hinduism on the other but cuts across both, as across all religions and spiritualities. But now I should like to direct what light may come from this approach upon the Christian claim to the 'specialness' of Jesus, without which *in some form* the gospel would cease to be itself or, for me at any rate, have anything worth continuing to believe in. I am concerned for my own sake, if for no one else's to clarify, complete and correct (to adapt Reinhold Niebuhr's formula[2]) what as a confessing Christian I want to say about Jesus as the Christ. And because I am deeply convinced of the approach we have been following, and not for purely defensive reasons, I regard it as vital to detach my *distinctive* understanding of the Christ from the *exclusivist* understanding which has been associated with one-eyed visions of the truth as it is in Jesus.

But first it will be well to remind ourselves that the divide between the emphasis upon uniqueness on the one hand and multiplicity on the other does not once again run down between the two ways of viewing the world of which we have spoken but across them. Each stresses both and has an equal, if different, concern for them. 'I, the Lord, am one' of the Hebraic and Islamic traditions or 'the one true God' *(ho monos alethinos theos)* of the Christian, on the one side, and, on the other, 'the one without a second' (*ekam evadvitiyam*) of the Vedantic or 'the One' (*to hen*) of the Neoplátonic – these affirmations represent for each approach to truth what Kierkegaard called the knot in the thread which prevents everything running through into nothingness. And unless 'the Christ', in whatever manifestation, reveals this one and the same reality he is not the Christ. The God who discloses himself in Jesus and the God who discloses himself in Krishna must be the same God, or he is no God – and there is no revelation at all. *Ultimately* for both sides there are not 'gods many and lords many' but one God, under whatever name, and indeed one Christ or *Logos*, however various the faces of his appearing. For the unity of the Christ, as the self-disclos-

[2] *The Nature and Destiny of Man* II, pp. 68, 85.

ure of the unconditional in the conditioned, is as fundamental
as the unity of God. If Jesus is the Christ, if, in other words,
God is to be met in him reconciling the world to himself, and
if Krishna or any other figure is an *avatara* of the 'All-highest
Brahman', 'the God of gods', then in the last analysis we
must be dealing with the same *Logos*, the same Christ. To
rest with an ultimate pluralism at this point is intolerable.
Hence the Hindu concern to absorb, to assimilate, which is
as powerful as any concern in the monotheisms of the West
to resist such absorption.

But, equally, both visions of the world recognize and insist
upon the revelation of God 'at sundry times and in divers
manners'. If he is to be seen in the face of Jesus or in Gautama
or Moses or Mohammed, it is because he has not left himself
without witness anywhere, indeed everywhere, else. The very
use of the *Logos* category, which transcends the Hebraic-
Hellenic divide, and any talk of the Wisdom or Spirit of God
as constitutive of all creation and history, presupposes the
validity of what the Fathers took over from pagan thought in
the concept of the *logos spermatikos*, the 'seeds of light'
implanted throughout the cosmos by the 'Source, Guide and
Goal of all that is' (Rom. 11.36). The recognition that the
light that enlightens every man found its focus and fulfilment
in Jesus (John 1.1–18) in no way cancels but on the contrary
crowns the revelation in and through the multiplicity of lights.
The unique does not absorb or exclude the many. Indeed the
greater the emphasis on history and historicity, the greater
the concern for the non-elimination of the particular. Time
and place matter. One cannot assert 'a local habitation and
a name' even for God, or supremely for God, without taking
seriously the significance of all that, in Hopkins' phrase, is
'counter, original, spare'[3]. The very stress on uniqueness, on
unrepeatability, on the denial that everything comes round
again or that all rivers lose themselves in the ocean, represents
an irreducible interest in multiplicity and particularity as the
presupposition of any 'once and for all' significance.

Moreover history, if genuine history, has the characteristic
of non-absoluteness, ambiguity and lack of finality. No his-

[3] 'Pied Beauty'.

torical statement admits of more than a greater degree of probability. The Christ therefore if he is genuinely the revelation of the unconditional *in* the conditioned, if he is not a docetic appearance *under the guise* of historical conditions, must be truly subject to them. This means that one cannot make any historical statements of Jesus, or anyone else, as the Christ which do not partake of this non-absolute character. Whatever one's faith-judgments, one cannot say of him *on the basis of historical evidence* that he was perfect, sinless, final, or absolutely unique.[4] All one can reasonably demand of the history to be able to affirm any of these things is that the credibility-gap be not too great – for instance, that he was not obviously, or even probably, a man with a police-record as long as your arm, or as mad as a hatter, or even just another Palestinian guerrilla. Precisely what gap is tolerable, how much one *needs* to know about him, or can know about him, or where the shoe pinches, will differ with each believer: he or she must decide whether Peter's question, 'Lord, to whom (else) shall we go?' (John 6.68), represents a live option. But that there is any exemption from 'historical risk' for someone who really believes in history or dares to assert that the Word was truly made *flesh* is, in my view, as against Tillich's, impossible.[5] Any stress therefore on the uniqueness or finality of the Christ will have to take into account the fact – which the Christian finds he has to live with much more than the Hindu – that the more one talks of a *once and for all* revelation or of an eschatological act of God *in* history the more paradoxical and problematic this appears.

On the one hand, any easy or tensionless syncretism which assimilates the manifestations of *Brahman* here, there and everywhere, or which accommodates temple, synagogue and church (or any other combination) simply as facets of the same truth, as, for instance, in the syncretistic painting which is given pride of place in the Ramakrishna Mission head-

---

[4] Cf. my essay, 'Need Jesus have been Perfect?', in *Christ, Faith and History*, ed. S. W. Sykes and J. P. Clayton, pp. 39–52.

[5] Cf. the discussion of this issue and the literature there referred to in my *Human Face of God*, pp. 125–7, and the debate between Tillich and Dodd related by Langdon Gilkey in Appendix I to F. W. Dillistone, *C. H. Dodd: Interpreter of the New Testament*, pp. 241–3.

quarters in Calcutta, is for him superficial. No progress in
dialogue is to be expected unless this is accepted. But equally
no progress in dialogue is to be expected unless from the
Christian side the ambiguity and tension is also accepted.
And this is where the fundamentalism of an absolutist, exclusivist or triumphalist assertion of the uniqueness of Jesus as
the Christ, as different in kind from any other manifestation
of the divine or exempt in principle from historical relativity,
has proved such a blockage. It is because a one-eyed approach
on each side has shown itself so unproductive that I believe
it is important to look for fresh light, and not merely to
concede points or stave off threats, in the wider context of
inter-faith dialogue.

Another way of stating the paradox is that if a manifestation
of the Christ is to be unique it must be exclusive, here but
not there, whereas if it is to be a manifestation of *the Christ*
it must be inclusive, enabling *all* things to cohere and hang
together (Col. 1.17). He must be *Unique and Universal*, to
use the excellent title of the introduction to Indian theology
I have already referred to. But there is a one-eyed exclusiveness *and* a one-eyed inclusiveness which are equally destructive, and from which we need to be released before progress
can be made.

On the one hand, it is possible so to elevate and isolate the
particular to the point at which the Christ becomes an anomalous exception, who is unique because he is abnormal, a
cuckoo in the human nest, without continuity with or relevance for the rest of history and mankind. As Norman Pittenger has observed, this is a subtle form of the heresy that
the Christ is not in the totality of his relationships, genetic
and environmental, fully and completely human:

> If we attempt to confine Incarnation to that individual in his
> supposed discreteness we shall find ourselves in the end in a
> position where we are in effect denying his genuine humanity
> and thus making of the Incarnation a docetic exception to human
> conditions, circumstances and situations.[6]

The 'here but not there' is viewed as having a purely negative

[6] *Christology Reconsidered*, p. 87; cf. pp. 125f.

relationship to the rest. And the world has been only too familiar with the particularism and the imperialism which making an 'ism' of the exclusive has engendered in the relationships of religions. It is a form of one-eyedness which has been especially characteristic of the West. Its limitations and short-comings, not to say sins and exploitations, have become evident enough, though the habits of mind, the resentments and the bad conscience it has left behind are still powerfully with us.[7] Can one, should one even presume to, speak any longer of the uniqueness or finality of Christ? There is an erosion of confidence and a residual legacy of guilt which is itself a potent factor of distortion. There is also the fear born of uncertainty that if this sort of exclusiveness is jettisoned then the uniqueness which it undoubtedly safeguarded is bound to be at risk. Hence a certain nervous shrillness is observable in the present debate within the church.

Meanwhile, from the other side, there is an emphasis on the non-exclusive, on the here but *also* there (and everywhere), which soon reduces revelation to sheer relativity and loses any criterion of discrimination. In John Hick's words,

> We should never forget that if the Christian gospel had moved east, into India, instead of west, into the Roman empire, Jesus' religious significance would probably have been expressed by hailing him within Hindu culture as a divine Avatar and within the Mahayana Buddhism which was then developing in India as a Bodhisattva, one who has attained to oneness with Ultimate Reality but remains in the human world out of compassion for mankind and to show others the way of life. These would have been the appropriate expressions, within those cultures, of the same spiritual reality.[8]

It is ironical that this paragraph should have been singled out for comment by two successive authors I was reading with totally opposite deductions, the one positive by Aelred Graham in 'Can We Learn from Eastern Religions?'[9] and the other negative by Norman Anderson in *The Mystery of the Incarnation*[10]. The former's question is significantly never

[7] Cf. Newbigin, *The Finality of Christ*, pp. 11–15.
[8] In *The Myth of God Incarnate*, ed. John Hick, p. 176.
[9] *The Ampleforth Journal* 83.2, 1978, p. 17.
[10] Op. cit., p. 63.

asked by the latter, even in a chapter on 'The Incarnation and Comparative Religion'. Anderson is nevertheless justified, I think, in querying in Hick's final sentence whether these would have been the *appropriate* expressions of the *same* reality. For it is easy to slip from a healthy recognition of undoubted relativity to the relativism of saying that truth is merely determined by geography and that in consequence any expressions of it are equally valid.

The hospitality of Hinduism to all (or most) religious insights *on its own terms*, which means plucking them from their roots in the historical particular, reflects just as one-eyed an approach as the attempt by the other traditions to transplant their own God, sods and all. The discipline of comparative religion and inter-faith dialogue should at any rate make us more aware of the blinkers on both sides. For syncretism is as much a socially conditioned phenomenon as the exclusivism it opposes, often with a similar, if more subtle, spiritual superiority, such as often one cannot help sensing, for instance, in Vivekananda and Radhakrishnan in their judgments of Christianity. So too is the relativism of many Christs, 'bubbling up' here, there and everywhere, of which one may only say that some are 'bigger' than others though all are equally destined to dissolve into steam. This may *look* less dogmatic than any notion of uniqueness or finality, but it is simply the product of a different myth, that of eternal recurrence rather than of purposive eschatology.

But with these preliminary warnings let us come back to the Christian claim for the uniqueness of Jesus as the Christ. What here is cultural conditioning, what is unexpendable content?

The inclusive and the exclusive

We may begin by observing the way in which within that tradition the significance of the 'once', of the decisive expression within history of the all-illuminating Christ, so easily gets transformed into a closed corpus of revelation, a deposit 'once and for all delivered to the saints', denying other revelation and even its own open-endedness. 'The one man' Jesus

Christ or 'the last Adam' is so defined as to rule out anything of significance outside or beyond him. He becomes the one who was everything and had everything – with the rest nowhere. From being *totus Christus* and *totus Deus*, the one who is utterly expressive of Godhead, through and through, so that in him there is no unChristlikeness at all, he becomes *totum Christi, totum Dei*, the exhaustive revelation and all-sufficient act, so that apart from him there is nothing of God and no Christlikeness at all. Further, the exclusivity of the Christ-event becomes transferred to the doctrine in which it is encapsulated and to the community by which it is transmitted. The strength of the centre is translated into the hardness of the edges. Both the deposit and its carrier become fixed, irreformable, infallible. Catholicity is defined by the static canon of *quod ubique, quod semper, quod ab omnibus creditum est* and the paradox of faith transposed into the obscurantism of *credo quia absurdum*. There is a glorying in 'our incomparable religion' (or liturgy, or whatever it may be), because in ignorance it never receives comparison or in insolence is placed beyond it. Christianity as a religion usurps the centrality of Christ (as in the original title even of Hick's book, *Christianity at the Centre*[11]). Then in the age of comparative religion it is proclaimed not to fall into the category of a 'religion'[12] at all: it is God's search for man rather than man's search for God. So far from welcoming and gathering into focus the light from all other sources, it presents itself, in practice if not in theory, as the denial of all other light and the assertion of darkness without. The inclusive Christ becomes the exclusive Christ, and witness to his all-embracing and saving significance appears as the unacceptable face of Catholic triumphalism or of Protestant particularism.

Yet this perversion is not mere perversity. It is the result of a sincere but one-eyed view both of scripture and of tradition. For there is a good deal in each which in isolation, and in the distortion that comes from isolation, can be made to

---

[11] Republished eight years later, in 1977, as *The Centre of Christianity*.

[12] W. Cantwell Smith, *The Meaning and End of Religion*, shows how this was itself a nineteenth-century Western designation foisted on the East. 'The term "Hinduism" is, in my judgment, a particularly false conceptualization' (p. 63).

feed it. Just as there is both a particularist and a universalist strain in the Old Testament, and in post-exilic Judaism the one is locked in conflict with the other, so, especially in the battle against Judaism and incipient Gnosticism, the New Testament witness includes what read like narrowly exclusivist as well as largely inclusivist statements. There are notoriously texts, especially in Acts and the Johannine writings and the Book of Revelation, which when taken out of context can be used to fuel the most intransigent response to light from other quarters. That there were men of that generation as of every other who under pressure reacted in a defensive and on occasion dismissive manner is not to be denied – and one could cite the greatest universalists, Paul and John, among them. Yet it is largely by ignoring their context that isolated verses can be wrested in this direction. One may illustrate this by reference to a few of those most commonly cited.

Thus in Acts 4.12 Peter is represented as saying of Jesus, 'There is no salvation in anyone else at all, for there is no other name under heaven granted to men by which we may be saved'. The first generalizing clause, which merely duplicates the sense, may not in any case on textual grounds be part of the original. But the real point is that the word for 'saved' here (and hence 'salvation') is exactly the same as that rendered three verses earlier in 4.9 by 'cured'. The context is not one of comparative religion but of faith-healing. The issue is 'by what power' the cripple is made 'completely well' (3.16). Is it by some innate power or godliness of the apostles (3.12) or is it by 'the name of Jesus, awakening faith' (3.16)? It is the same question that Jesus himself faced in the Beelzebub controversy (Matt. 12.22–30; Mark 3.22–7; Luke 11.14–23), except that there his opponents were charging him with using not simply his own power but that of Satan. It is an issue far removed from whether there is any 'saving' revelation of God outside Jesus. In fact in the Beelzebub controversy Jesus himself takes it for granted that God's healing power over the devils is at work through others, including his opponents ('by whom do your sons cast them out?'): he claims no exclusive powers for himself. Acts 4.12 should never be quoted in the debate on comparative religion.

It is the same with one of the most abused texts in the Fourth Gospel. In John 10.8 Jesus is represented as saying: 'All who came before me are thieves and robbers'. Here in fact there is very serious doubt about the true text. The words 'before me' are missing from a weighty consensus of early manuscripts and versions and are bracketed in the latest editions of the Greek New Testament. I am convinced indeed that the saying has nothing to do with discrediting every previous revelation of God in Judaism, though doubtless the words 'before me' were added in the interests of anti-Jewish apologetic (or simply to ease the difficulty of the Greek without them). In fact in this gospel Jesus's precursors, like Abraham, Moses and Isaiah, are consistently represented as witnessing to him (John 1.45; 5.46; 8.56; 12.41). Still less can this verse be used to eliminate any authentic manifestations of God outside Judaism. The contrast in the passage (10.1–18), and it is a strong one, is between Jesus as the authentic shepherd of Israel and those who 'climb up by some other way', claimants to the leadership of God's people who try to enter and control the sheep-fold by force. These are the 'thieves and robbers', and the word 'robber' (*lestes*) is that which John uses of the insurrectionist Barabbas (18.40) and Josephus later of the Zealot revolutionaries. The background of the passage is the denunciation, especially in Ezekiel 34, of the self-serving shepherds of Israel and the promise that God himself would provide his people with a faithful shepherd. Again it has nothing to do with the comparative religion debate.

Much the same must be said of another Johannine text which is frequently put to exclusivist use: 'Jesus said: "I am the way, the truth and the life: no one comes to the Father but by me" '(14.6). The context here is Thomas's question about how the disciples can know where Jesus is going, and therefore how they can know the way. The answer is that he is going to the Father, and since they know him they have no need to ask further with Philip, 'Show us the Father': to have seen Jesus is to have seen the Father (14.1–11). The point the evangelist is making, to use our earlier distinction, is that

Jesus as the Christ is *totus Deus*: the Father is perfectly reflected in him, he is God 'all through'. There is no suggestion in the context that he is claiming to be *totum Dei*, that outside him there is no truth or life to be found. The assurance is that in him truth and life *are* to be found: therefore there is no cause for anxious fears.

Nevertheless one may use this text to make the point that empirically speaking the way into the understanding of God as *Abba*, Father, is characteristically and distinctively (though not exclusively) the contribution of the Christian revelation.[13] Perhaps I may quote again at this point some further words of Hick, since he can hardly be accused of exclusivism:

> No man cometh to the Father – that is, to God as Father – except through the Christ, in whom as Son the love of the Father is fully revealed. But millions of men and women may in Buddhism have come to God as release out of suffering into *Nirvana*; or in Islam to God as holy and sovereign will addressing the Arab peoples through Mohammed; or in Hinduism to God as many-sided source and meaning of life. And further, it may be that Christ (God as personal love) is also present in these other religions, and their several awarenesses of God likewise present to some extent in Christianity.[14]

Father and son

This provides a way into the positive consideration of what is the 'speciality' that the Christian wishes to assert of Jesus as the Christ – to use the term Pittenger prefers[15] to the ambiguous world 'uniqueness', since in one sense everyone of us is unique and unrepeatable and in another it can mean purely anomalous. For there can be no question of the centrality both to the synoptic and to the Johannine record of the Father-Son language to describe Jesus's awareness of God and of his own relationship to him. So it will be good to start

[13] Cf. the classic study of 'Abba' by J. Jeremias, *The Prayers of Jesus*, pp. 11–65.
[14] 'The Reconstruction of Christian Belief', *Theology* 73, 1970, pp. 404f. Cf. also the whole discussion in which I cited this in my *Human Face of God*, pp. 220–30.
[15] 'Christology in Process Theology', *Theology* 80, 1977, pp. 187–93 (192); cf. his *Christology Reconsidered*, ch. 6.

by grounding what we have to say in an analysis of it.

This language is in the New Testament, as previously in the Old, in origin parabolic. It uses the intimacy of human relationships to convey the ultimacy of that which lies at the heart of all things. Thus Jesus says: 'Is there a father among you who will offer his son a snake . . . ? How much more will the heavenly Father . . . ?' (Luke 11.11–13). Jeremias has convincingly shown[16] that the seemingly ontological and to us almost 'Nicene' language set so surprisingly on Jesus's lips in one of the earliest gospel sources, the common material behind Matthew and Luke, is similarly parabolic. In the words, 'No one knows the Son but the Father, and no one knows the Father but the Son' (Matt. 11.27 = Luke 10.22), the 'the' is not metaphysical but generic. It is the same 'the' as in other parabolic sayings, such as 'The sower went forth to sow' (Mark 4.3) or 'The grain of wheat remains solitary unless it falls into the ground and dies' (John 12.24). English idiom here requires the indefinite article, 'a'. So this saying means: 'Just as only a father really knows his son, so only a son really knows his father.' Jesus is indeed using this picture from everyday life to describe the intimacy of the *abba* relationship that he himself is claiming with God (Mark 14.36) and which he teaches his disciples to take upon their lips (Luke 11.2; cf.the memory of it, still in Aramaic, in Rom. 8.15 and Gal. 4.6). He is *'the* son' *par eminence*, and this language is used of him in all layers of the gospel tradition to designate his 'special relationship' to God. The speciality it implies is brought out in the parable of the wicked husbandmen (Mark 12.1–12 and pars) where the son in contrast to the servants is heir to the estate, or in the Johannine saying where the son, in the same contrast with the servants, enjoys permanent status in the home and the freedom of his father's house (John 8.35; cf. 15.15).

In fact the parabolic basis of this language is nowhere clearer than in the Fourth Gospel, where again by transposing from the definite to the indefinite article Dodd has laid bare[17]

---

[16] Op. cit., pp. 45–52.

[17] 'A Hidden Parable in the Fourth Gospel', *More New Testament Studies*, pp. 30–40.

what he calls the parable of the apprentice-son in 5.19f.: 'A son can do nothing on his own; he does only what he watches his father doing: what father does, son does; for a father loves his son and shows him all he does.' Indeed the evangelist's first introduction of it in 1.14 is as a simile from human relationships. This has been obscured from English readers by capitalization and definite articles that have no place in the Greek, which runs literally: 'glory as of a father's only son'. From the use at that time of the word *doxa* to mean reflection[18] this almost certainly in my judgment means that just as an only son is the very spit and image of his father so the *Logos* incarnate is the perfect reflection, a mirror-image, of God's being.[19] The point here of 'only' son is not to indicate exclusiveness, but, as in Hebrew usage, to signify 'beloved' (*agapetos*), the one who is the apple of his father's eye (cf. Mark 1.11 and pars; 9.7 and pars; 12.6; Luke 20.13). Indeed the term *monogenes*, 'only' son, like *prototokos*, 'first-born' (Exod. 4.22; Jer. 31.9; etc.), had already been applied in Judaism to Israel (Ps. Sol. 18.4). And when God says to Israel, 'You only have I known' (in the same intimate sense of 'no one knows the Son except the Father') 'of all the families of the earth' (Amos 3.2), it certainly does not for the prophet imply an exclusive relationship. For ' "Are you not like the Ethiopians to me, O people of Israel?" says the Lord. "Did I not bring up Israel from the land of Egypt, and the Philistines from Caphtor and the Syrians from Kir?" ' (Amos 9.7).

The simile or parable of the intimacy of a son's relationship to his father is of course 'allegorized' by the evangelists to speak of Jesus as 'the Son' and God as 'the Father' very early in the gospel tradition (Matt. 11.27 = Luke 10.22; Mark 13.32). And, in John, only a few verses later on in the prologue we have: 'No one has ever seen God; but the only Son, he who is nearest to the Father's heart, he has made him known' (1.18). In fact by far the weightiest manuscript tradition here has, in place of *monogenes huios*, 'the only Son', *monogenes*

---

[18] As e.g. in I Cor. 11.7; II Cor.8.23, NEB margin.
[19] Cf. Heb.1.3: 'He reflects the glory of God and bears the very stamp of his nature.'

theos, which the NEB margin paraphrases as 'the only one, himself God'. For the phrase is so difficult as almost to be untranslatable. That the *Logos* should be *theos*, 'what God was' (John 1.1, NEB), is no problem. But the expression 'only begotten God' is so odd and the context seems so strongly to demand reference to 'the Son' as correlate of 'the Father's heart' that I am inclined to judge that the RSV and NEB are right still to prefer *huios* to *theos* against the weight of the manuscript evidence and to attribute the other reading to a slip in dictation or transcription. But, whichever is correct, for John the Son is the one who is the expression (literally the 'exegesis') of the Father, because he is closest to him: he is 'with God' (1.1), he shares and reflects his 'glory' (1.14; 17.5), he is privy to his 'name' or inmost nature (17.6). 'He who has come from God has seen the Father, and he alone' (6.46; cf. 7.29; 16.27; 17.8). No story could apparently be more 'exclusive'. Yet this disclosure of 'what I saw in my Father's presence' (8.38) is described by Jesus himself as the work of '*a man* who told you the truth *as I heard it from God*' (8.40). And to be 'a man from God' (*para theou*) (9.16,33), as to be 'sent from God' or 'come from God', is not in this Gospel confined to Jesus. It is applied to John the Baptist (1.6), and in its widest sense is equated with being 'a prophet' (9.17) and indeed with 'anyone who is devout and obeys his will' (9.31). Even the attempt to reserve the preposition *ek* (out of) God, as opposed to *para* or *apo* (from), to designate 'unique origination in the being of God'[20] must be judged to fail. The three prepositions are used apparently with mere stylistic variation in 16.27, 28 and 30, and above all *ek tou theou* which in 8.42 is applied to Jesus is five verses later applied to any man and *should* be true even of the Jews.[21] If Jesus is unique it is not because abnormally he does not share a human origin or the relationship to God potentially open to all other men. It is because he alone is normal, truly 'son' to the Father: 'He who has God for his father listens to the words of God. You are not God's children (*ek*

[20] Dodd, *The Interpretation of the Fourth Gospel*, pp. 259f.
[21] For a fuller review of this and similar evidence, cf. *The Human Face of God*, pp. 172–8.

tou theou); that is why you do not listen' (8.47).

Nowhere more than in the Gospel of John, which can scarcely be accused of having a low Christology, is sonship used in its fundamental Hebraic sense to designate not absolute status but functional relationship. To be a son is essentially to show the character, to reproduce the thought and action, of another, whether it be Abraham, the devil or God. To claim sonship to God is therefore a sign not of blasphemy but of fidelity. In a passage which is thoroughly rabbinic in its exegetical methods Jesus turns their own scriptures against the Jews and concludes:

> Why do you charge me with blasphemy because I, consecrated and sent into the world by the Father, said 'I am a son of God' (*huios theou*, without articles). If I am not acting as my Father would, do not believe me. But if I am, accept the evidence of my deeds, even if you do not believe me, so that you may recognize and know that the Father is in me, and I in the Father (10.34–8).

It is lack of moral correspondence which would really discredit his claim to be God's son. And this is the context in which Jesus says, 'My Father and I are one' (10.30). It is not – and here Appasamy and earlier Ram Mohan Roy and Keshab Chandra Sen and other Indians were quite correct – because of some metaphysical identity which renders him entirely anomalous, but because 'I always do what is acceptable to him' (8.29): 'My deeds done in my Father's name are my credentials' (10.24). Similarly, when later he claims that 'anyone who has seen me has seen the Father', it is not because he and the Father are ontologically indistinguishable but because, paradoxically, 'I am *not* myself the source of the words I speak to you: it is the Father who dwells in me doing his own work' (14.9). For in the one who is utterly and completely 'son', nothing of self gets in the way: God simply shines through him. For this reason he is the very mirror-image of the Father (1.14,18), and indeed himself *theos* (1.1). It is not because, as the Jews distortingly assert, 'You, a mere man, claim to *be* God' (10.33), but because as a man he is totally transparent to Another, who is greater than himself (14.28) and indeed than all (10.29). Everything the Father has is his *because* everything he has is the Father's (17.10): as Son he is and can do nothing 'of himself' (5.19; cf. 7.18). In Heinrich Zahrnt's succinct phrase, 'Jesus Christ is the Son because he alone allows God really to be his Father.'[22]

In all this the Fourth Gospel is saying nothing essentially different from the Synoptists. For they too proclaim Jesus as 'the man who lived God', who dared to stand and speak and act *in loco Dei*, as his *shaliach* or representative.[23] It is no different either from the picture presented by the Epistle to the Hebrews with its characteristic use of 'son' without the article (also first introduced, in 1.1f., in comparison with God's servants the prophets who were not 'heirs') to designate Jesus as the one who *alone* stood where *all* men should stand and who could thus communicate his unique, but universal, relationship to his brothers. Nor does it differ from Paul's understanding of Christ as the true Adam, the archetypal 'son of God' (cf. Luke 3.38), who by adoption incorporates all men into his filial obedience. Here I have concentrated on the Johannine presentation, partly because I am persuaded that it is as near to source as any other, *as well as being* the most developed and profound, but also because it is constantly asserted that it *is* saying something very different from the other witnesses – namely, that Jesus was not really a human being at all but God in human form walking this earth, or several inches above it, without leaving a footprint. And it is this picture that has so often been isolated and distorted by Gnostic and by Hindu interpreters.

Pre-existence and incarnation

But in fairness nowhere, I believe, has it been more distorted, even if one discounts the docetic excesses, than in the interpretation which has been built upon it in the main stream of the church's doctrinal development. Indeed the majority of exegetes have seen the signs of the development to which I am about to refer within the Fourth Gospel and other parts

---

[22] *The Historical Jesus*, p. 142.
[23] For this side of the evidence I would refer again to my *The Human Face of God*, pp. 190–4.

of the New Testament itself. They may be right, though I personally believe that the interpretation is brought to the texts by reading them with the presuppositions and questions of a later age. The prologue to the Fourth Gospel, like comparable passages both in Paul and the Epistle to the Hebrews (e.g., Phil. 2.5–11; Col. 1.15–19; Heb. 1.1–4), has been seen as presenting the descent of a supernatural being discontinuous in origin from the mass of humanity he came to save. He is unique because he was *not* one of them at all but underneath, as it were, was the Second Person of the Trinity. '*The* son of God' (with a small 's'), the man who alone truly is what all other men are called to be, becomes transposed as 'God the Son'. The one who, in Theodore of Mopsuestia's phrase, discloses God '*as* in a son',[24] or, as Ignatius put it earlier,[25] *anthropinos*, humanly, in a person of flesh and blood, becomes God visiting the earth in a Person of the Trinity – and very problematically human. This way of putting it certainly safeguards the New Testament witness that Jesus was *monogenes* or 'only' son, a term which as I said, means originally what Paul calls 'the son of his love' (Col. 1.13); but it does so at the cost of denying him in the fullest sense as 'first-born' (*prototokos*), 'the eldest among a large family of brothers' (Rom. 8.29). The horizontal nexus with the rest of humanity which in the New Testament is never at issue becomes questionable: he is unlike his brethren not only in sin but in origin.

It is important to see precisely what is happening here and where the proper objection to it lies. It is not, as the authors of *The Myth of God Incarnate* represent it, that the doctrine is heightened, that Jesus is deified from having been simply 'a man approved of God' (Acts 2.22). I would in principle agree entirely with C. F. D. Moule in his careful study, *The Origin of Christology*,[26] that the course of Christian thinking is much more accurately depicted as the drawing out of what was implicit from the beginning than as the evolving of divinity out of a primitive adoptionism. For some of the highest

---

[24] *De Incarn.* 7; cf. again John 1.14.
[25] *Ad Eph.* 19.3.
[26] See especially ch. 1.

Christology comes at the beginning. Of course, as Moule
readily agrees, particular forms of expression, like that of pre-
existence, represent developments, though again early developments. But my concern here is with how the concept of
pre-existence is to be understood.

As I read the evidence (and this much is scarcely in dispute), it begins within post-exilic Judaism as the personification of certain attributes, activities or aspects of God, such
as Wisdom, Spirit, Word, which are conceived as being 'with
him' from the beginning and operating as agents of creation.
These personifications represent metaphor or myth: they do
not refer to real entities, let alone to individual persons. The
distinctive affirmation of the Christian faith is that this 'self-
expressive activity of God', as Pittenger characterizes the
Logos (but it would cover the other ways of putting it), is
personalized, in the strict sense of being made a person, of
becoming, or being embodied in, a historical individual who
perfectly incarnates or enmans it. It is not so much that Jesus
becomes God as that the reality of God, the eternal divine
activity of personalizing love, comes into being and reaches
its supreme manifestation as this man. This, as G. W. H.
Lampe insists,[27] is the decisive new factor. It is because the
Logos is embodied no longer simply in nature or history or
even in a people but as a person that the development of
which we have spoken becomes possible. *The individual personality of this historical Jesus is retrojected on to a pre-
existent heavenly Person*[28] – as it is also projected in his 'post-
existence'. Personified pre-existence becomes personal pre-
existence.[29] This supernatural Person is then seen, by revers-
ing the process, as the subject of all that the historical indi-

[27] *God as Spirit*, pp. 39f.
[28] Lampe indeed would see this development as reflected already in John, as in
Paul and the writer to the Hebrews. I would judge that it is we who read it back
into them by viewing the New Testament authors through the spectacles of the
patristic age. See my *Human Face of God*, ch. 5, and G. B. Caird, 'The Development
of the Doctrine of Christ in the New Testament', in *Christ for Us Today*, ed. Norman
Pittenger, pp. 66–80. But whether it occurred in or after the New Testament is for
our present purposes a secondary issue.
[29] For an interesting discussion of this issue within Indian theology, see W. Roy
Pape, 'Keshub Chunder Sen's Doctrine of Christ and the Trinity: A Rehabilitation',
IJT 25, 1976, pp. 55–71, especially 59–64, where he argues that Sen held this position
and is now being vindicated.

vidual was and did. The end-term of this is the patristic doctrine of *anhypostasia* or *enhypostasia*, namely, that Jesus had no personhood or *hypostasis* of his own, which was replaced or constituted by that of the Second Person of the Trinity assuming a second, human, nature as well as his own.[30]

The strained sense, not to say travesty, which this has made of the biblical evidence, quite apart from the internal difficulties of the notion of an 'impersonal' humanity which is still genuinely human, has recently been exposed once again by Lampe with professional expertise. He shows how this way of putting it, so far from constituting the bulwark of catholic orthodoxy,[31] is a liability to the central truth which it purports to protect.[32] Where, however, I would venture to differ from him (though from conversation I think we should be very close) is whether the transposing of a *Logos*-son Christology into a Spirit Christology, for which he argues, in itself affects

[30] I would agree with P. Schoonenberg, *The Christ*, pp. 54–66, 80–91, that if one has to use these categories, the biblical evidence is best safeguarded by standing the traditional doctrine on its head and saying that it is the Word that was anhypostatic (i.e. not a person) until it took individuality in the man Jesus Christ. He has since modified his position somewhat (the details are too technical for our present discussion), but he tells me in a letter of 3 October 1978 that he still wishes to maintain 'two important points: (1) that Jesus is a human person; (2) that the *Logos* is not personal before the incarnation.'

[31] Bonhoeffer described it as 'the last refuge of docetism' (*Christology*, p. 81), and most recently J. P. Mackey as 'the least possible form of Apollinarianism, or the most tolerable, whichever expression is preferred' (*Jesus: The Man and the Myth*, p. 240). It is still vigorously defended by E. L. Mascall in *Theology and the Gospel of Christ*, and for those who find the exercise credible, no one does the theological mathematics better.

For an interesting Indian equivalent which sought to translate catholic orthodoxy but can scarcely, as Boyd says (*Indian Christian Theology*, pp. 79f.), escape the charge of Apollinarianism, cf. the attempt of Brahmabandhav Upadhyaya to present Christ as the *Logos*-God acting directly upon the five 'sheaths' that make up man without any medium of individuality. Cf. J. Mattam, 'Interpreting Christ to India Today: The Calcutta School', *IJT* 23, 1974, p. 196.

[32] It needs to be stressed that one is not committed to this way of putting it by the Chalcedonian Definition itself, but only by the interpretation given to it by Cyril and the Alexandrians. The Antiochenes vigorously repudiated it. In fact the Alexandrian school shifted the emphasis of Christian theology from a *Logos*-son to a *Logos*-flesh Christology. It was the Antiochenes like Theodore and Nestorius who insisted that in the incarnation God took 'a man', as opposed to the *Logos* assuming an 'impersonal' flesh – though the presupposition which they also shared, of a pre-existent Son in heaven, never allowed them to shake off the suspicion that they were teaching 'two sons'.

the main issue. Without denying the many fruitful insights
that come by seeing Christ as the supreme expression of the
Spirit of God, I would question whether 'son' language is *per
se* the root of the trouble. The manifestation of the divine 'as
in a son', where, as Lampe rightly says, the sonship of Jesus
'means that he is truly and fully human: man as the Creator
has designed him, that is, in unbroken fellowship with God'[33]
– this is after all the very core of the New Testament message.
What goes wrong is when sonship which is 'in the last resort
a relationship of a human being to God'[34] is projected back
so that 'the Logos becomes Jesus writ large, a divine Jesus in
heaven before he came down to earth'.[35] There is in my
judgment nothing against retaining 'son' as the controlling
category of our Christology, though from its very metaphor
it is obviously more susceptible to personalization than 'spirit'
or 'word'. Indeed I believe that we must preserve its centrality
as expressing better than any other the *human* 'face' of God,
so long as we do not hypostasize it into a divine Person who
thereby becomes the subject of Jesus's human nature. We
then get the charade of the prayer of the human Jesus, 'Not
my will but thine be done', being transposed, as Lampe puts
it, into a debate within the *Logos*: 'Not my human will, but
my divine will be done'.[36]

While differing but marginally from Lampe in wishing to
hold on to sonship as the primary category in Christology, I
should wish to differ more seriously with the authors of *The
Myth of God Incarnate* in a strong desire to retain that of
'incarnation'. To call their opening chapter 'Christianity
without Incarnation?' seems rather like entitling a book
'Christianity without the Bible?' when you mean 'Christianity
without biblicism'. To allow the term 'incarnation' (in any
strict sense[37]) to be equated, and then discarded, with a par-

---

[33] *God as Spirit*, p. 23. He concurs with me in seeing this as the meaning of his
being in the 'form' (or image) of God in Phil. 2.6.

[34] Op. cit., p. 139.

[35] Op. cit., p. 39.

[36] Op. cit., p. 143.

[37] Maurice Wiles concedes a 'looser' sense, to mean simply that 'man's approach
to God is through the physical world rather than by escape from it' (op. cit., ed.
John Hick, p. 1); but that could apply equally to Judaism.

ticular myth or metaphysic of God's self-revelation in Jesus
as the Christ is surely to throw out the baby with the bath-
water. The word, to be sure, has nothing sacrosanct about it.
It *can*, as its etymology suggests, be limited to designate the
coating in flesh of a pre-existent spiritual being; but there is
no reason why it should, any more than that it should signify
the embodiment of God's loving purpose. I believe in fact
that it represents one of the bed-rock categories of distinctively
Christian truth and should be redeemed from dependence
upon any particular metaphor or interpretation. For it focuses
attention on what Augustine again in his day put his finger
on as being unique to the gospel, namely that 'the Word was
made *flesh*', bone of our bone. And this is the affirmation that
marks Christianity off also from Judaism or Islam, Hinduism,
Buddhism or Gnosticism. Without it Christianity is nothing.[38]
But how one expresses it is entirely secondary and infinitely
adaptable.

No one could be more insistent than I in wishing to detach
it from any supranaturalist or interventionist schema.[39] If it
helps to say not that God comes down or comes in but that
he comes through or even comes out in Jesus, fine. The
essential thing is that in this man, the invisible divine reality
becomes visible, surfaces, breaks through, so that in him we
meet and are met not *just* by one more fellow human being
– though we are indeed – but by the life and power and love
which 'moves the sun and other stars'. This is what the
prologue to the Gospel of John is asserting and what the noun
'incarnation' which has entered the language from his *sarx
egeneto*, stands for, though Pittenger's 'enmanment' is probably open to less misunderstanding. Better still perhaps, with
its background in Barth's rich understanding of 'the humanity
of God' is 'the humanization of God'. Defending this term,
Choan-Seng Song from Taiwan writes:

In our judgment, the phrase 'the humanization of God' expresses

---

[38] Cf. K. Leech, 'Believing in the Incarnation', *Theology* 79, 1976, pp. 68–76.
[39] For my Christology as a whole I must refer once more to *The Human Face of
God*; also to Pittenger's classic but neglected work, *The Word Incarnate*, which
retains in its title the same emphasis, while in its treatment abjuring all that I have
been arguing against.

more adequately what the time-honoured theological term 'incarnation' intends to convey. This is especially true in today's Asia, and for that matter in the Third World. Although the term incarnation has its biblical origin in John 1.14 where it is said that the Word became flesh, it has a certain metaphysical overtone. Consequently, the dynamic of the Greek verb *egeneto* in *ho logos sarx egeneto* tends to get lost sight of in the use of the term incarnation. . . . But without taking into serious account the verb *egeneto*, how is it possible for us to comprehend the mystery of God and man becoming one in Jesus Christ?[40]

But, whichever term is used, what it is affirming is that this fully personal manifestation of the *Logos* 'as in a son' is God for us, Emmanuel. What the Word was God was: to have seen him is to have seen the Father.

Perhaps the essentials can be communicated in words of another Eastern Christian that avoid the dangers of the personification which has crept in through the Western categories of *hypostasis* and *persona*. He was a Hindu convert for whom Robin Boyd came to have a deep admiration, Dhanjibhai Fakirbhai (1895–1967). Basing his interpretation on a passage of the Upanishads which has interesting affinities with St John's prologue,[41] he puts it thus:

> *Prajnana*, the primeval intelligence, is the power which creates, maintains and inspires the world and human beings. *Prajnana* is power and wisdom, is the Word of God (*Sabda-Brahman*), is God himself – *Brahman*. This Word of God, *Prajnana*, took a body in the man Jesus. As the heat of the sun's light, according to the *Brahma Sutra*, is no different from the heat of the disc of the sun itself, so this incarnate *Prajnana*, the *Avatara*, is fully God.

[40] *Christian Mission in Reconstruction*, p. 217. He relates this also to the continuing mission of God. In words that accord closely with Thomas's *Salvation and Humanisation*, he says: 'God humanises himself to bring humanisation into the world. Thus, the humanisation of God is the salvation of the world...The mission of God begins with humanisation and achieves its purpose in humanisation. In short, salvation is humanisation' (p. 217).

[41] 'That which is heart, mind, consciousness, perception, discrimination, intelligence, wisdom, insight...all these, indeed, are appellations of *Prajnana* ("primeval intelligence"). He is *Brahman*...All this is guided by *Prajnana*, is based on *Prajnana* The world is guided by *Prajnana* . . . . *Brahman* is *Prajnana*' (*Aitareya Up.* 3.1.2f.). Remarkably, this passage is not included either in Zaehner's *Hindu Scriptures* or in Panikkar's *Vedic Experience*.

In comment Boyd adds: 'That, I believe, says something which a Hindu can understand, and which – if he does understand it – will take him very close to the orthodox doctrine of the incarnation of the Logos.'[42] It is to be observed that Dhanjibhai does not say that this *Prajnana* 'took the body of the man Jesus' but that this divine guiding creative Intelligence 'took body', became embodied, 'in the man Jesus': he was the fullest incorporation and expression of it.

In his earlier days[43] Hick expressed this essential conviction by the statement that Jesus is of one love (*homoagape*) with the Father. It is not simply that in him we see a love which is *like* that of God (*homoiagape*), but that in him God is acting, reconciling the world to himself (II Cor. 5.19). Austin Farrer expressed the same thing when he said that, for the Christian, Jesus is not just a man doing human things divinely, but a man doing divine things humanly. That I believe is the heart of the distinctively Christian claim, though I think we should recognize that virtually none of the church Fathers would have put it this way. They would have started at the other end and said that Christ was God doing divine things humanly, or human things divinely, according to the 'nature' through which the 'Person' was conceived as operating. They did their Christology 'from above', whereas I am convinced that we must do ours, like the first disciples, 'from below', proceeding with Augustine (and subsequently Luther) 'from Christ as man to Christ as God'.[44] This involves a readiness to sit loose to almost everything in the *superstructure* of traditional doctrine – divine Persons, two natures, impersonal humanity and the rest. But I believe that we must hold to the root, and in this sense be radical, if we are to be honest to what the New Testament presents of Jesus as 'the human face of God'. Whatever our stretching-points, our sticking-point must be the reality of this man as embodying, fleshing out, the saving disclosure and act of God.

[42] *India and the Latin Captivity of the Church*, p. 109. He is summarizing Dhanjibhai's last and still unpublished work *Adhyatma Darshana (A Vision of Spirituality)*.
[43] 'Christology at the Cross-roads', in *Prospect for Theology: Essays in Honour of H. H. Farmer,* edited by F. G. Healey, ch. 6.
[44] *Serm.* 261.7.

It is to express the divine initiative in this self-revelation, the marvel that God first loved us, not we him (I John 4.19), that the New Testament writers, and particularly Paul and John, speak of the Father 'sending' his Son or of the Son 'coming down' from heaven. The Christ is indeed 'from above' (John 3.31; 8.23) and not simply 'from below', though he is *also* from Nazareth, out of the womb of Israel and the family of man, 'of one stock' with those whom he sanctifies (Heb. 2.11). He 'belongs' in the bosom of the Father, his 'home' is in heaven. As Son he enjoys the freedom of his Father's house; he lives and speaks from source, 'with authority', *ex-ousia*, out of the heart of being. But this does not mean that his humanity was pre-existent any more than that of any other individual – except in so far as the stuff out of which *homo sapiens* is wrought reaches back to the very beginnings of creation (and that for us may be the heart of what the gospel genealogies are affirming in saying that he is 'son of Adam, Son of God' [Luke 3.38]). What it does mean is that the 'glory', the self-giving *agape*, which this man mirrors is 'something far more deeply interfused' than anything even 'whose dwelling is the light of setting suns . . . and in the mind of man'.[45] Its dwelling, in Johannine terms, is 'with the Father before the world began' (John 17.5). Such eternally is what this human life reveals in all its temporal particularity.

Defining without confining

That this is the language of poetry, word-picture, myth, and is not to be taken literally, is so obvious as hardly to be worth saying – though it is important to say it, since myth is a profound form of truth, and not the opposite of truth as the deliberate antithesis of the titles *The Myth of God Incarnate* and *The Truth of God Incarnate*[46] would suggest. But, as Maurice Wiles rightly says in the former book, 'Simply to call something a myth does not of course in itself solve anything.'[47]

[45] W. Wordsworth, 'Tintern Abbey'.
[46] The holding together of fact and myth as equally essential forms of truth is the strength of Mackey's *Jesus: The Man and the Myth*.
[47] Op. cit., p. 165.

It certainly does not of itself settle the question of the uniqueness of Christ in relation to other religions, and it was simplistic of that symposium by mixing the two issues to suggest that it could. Certainly, the two are connected, in that if one does *not* recognize the language of 'incarnation' as language of myth but takes it literally, with either a biblical or a doctrinal fundamentalism, then one will be forced to conclude that it was a visitation of God 'in Person' different *in kind* from any disclosure through other religions. Yet to recognize the language as myth does not mean that it *cannot* be interpreted in an exclusivist manner: myth can depict any truth one wishes to assert. Nor, *per contra*, does it mean that it cannot be used, as some of the essayists seem to me to use it, to give expression to a reductionist Christology which leaves little distinctive content to the Christian faith at all. That issue still remains to be settled on its own merits.

But it is nevertheless important, and in this *The Myth of God Incarnate* performed a useful service, to insist that it cannot be resolved *a priori* from above, by invoking absolutist categories of a once-and-for-all intervention which dispense one from having to enter the field of invidious comparisons with other religions.[48] That is to prejudge the issue by reading in an exclusivist interpretation from the beginning, which of course can readily be done by a one-eyed and uncritical use of scripture. Yet if we do not seek to pre-empt the question 'from above', how do we proceed to work through it *a posteriori*, from below? This will inevitably be a more tentative and extended task and one in which the contribution of other faiths and spiritualities must be welcomed. For in its cultural isolation in the period of Christendom, when it has largely 'had it to itself', Christian theology has for the most part not been compelled to give a thought-out answer on equal terms for the uniqueness of the claim that it makes. And many, especially among the young, have now lost the confidence that it can, or even that it should, be done. This is where

---

[48] Michael Goulder, in *The Myth of God Incarnate*, ed. John Hick, p. 57, tries to have it both ways, by abjuring absolutist categories but also bowing out from 'the distasteful and unprofitable task' of comparing Jesus with the leaders of other world religions. He falls back on saying, 'Mine is a confessional statement.'

dialogue and the presence of a second 'eye' on truth is a
positive and indeed a vital asset. Otherwise we shall be shut
up to the familiar sterile debate between exclusivist present-
ations and those which effectively empty the Christian faith
of anything unique or historically decisive.

The larger question of what Indian theology, in conjunction
with liberation theology, black theology, women's theology
and the rest, may have to offer to reshaping Christian doctrine
as a whole must be left till the next chapter. But an example
of how East and West may meet creatively at the point of the
uniqueness of Christ is to be found in the symposium I mentioned earlier, *Unique and Universal*. In the chapter specifically devoted to the 'Uniqueness and Universality of Christ',[49]
J. A. G. van Leeuwen, the only European contributor, seeks
to marry the insights of recent Dutch Catholic theology with
those of Indian thought. He writes:

> The uniqueness of Christ can only be established via his human-
> ity. . . . The divinity must be perceptible *in* his humanity
> itself . . . We do not have to accept a divine personality coming in
> from the outside in order to safeguard his unique 'image-hood' of
> God.

Jesus as the Christ is 'the image of the invisible God' (Col.
1.25) precisely as by the self-emptying of his individual ego
(*aham* or *anavam*) in utterly powerless humility he allows
God to be everything. There is nothing of himself to prevent
his being totally transparent to the Father. The Western
emphasis on the I, even of the I-Thou relation, can get in the
way. And for the elaboration of this, with its clear affinities
with the *advaitic* approach, van Leeuwen quotes the work of
the Indian Christian Vengal Chakkarai.[50]

Chakkarai indeed merits more extended treatment than we
can give him here. His Christology is very much in line with
what I have been delineating.

---

[49] Op. cit., ed. J. B. Chethimattam, pp. 144–54.

[50] With Chenchiah, Chakkarai (1880–1958), also a member of the legal profession
and a Hindu convert, was one of the group of Madras theologians (the 'Rethinking'
group) responsible for the volume in reply to Kraemer, *Rethinking Christianity in
India*. For his thought, cf. P. T. Thomas, *The Theology of Chakkarai*, and Boyd,
Indian Christian Theology, ch. 9.

We see God with the face of Jesus. To the ordinary and unso-
phisticated consciousness there is a black veil God would seem
to have cast over his face. But now that Jesus has removed the
veil, we behold the face of God himself. . . . Whom we call God
stands behind Jesus, and it is Jesus who gives, as it were, colour,
light and *rupa*[form] to God.

In the picture of Jesus the express image of the Invisible has
come out. . . . It is a picture in which the Lord of the universe
has found his own soul. The Painter and the picture are one.[51]

But they are one because in Jesus humanity is uniquely transparent to divinity.[52] Interpreting Chakkarai, Boyd writes:

We must not think of Jesus as 'metaphysically' one with the
Father in any monist sense, but on the other hand we should not
look on him as a 'mere' man, for he is the True Man who lives
in complete communion with the Father. Chakkarai interprets
Jesus' sinlessness in terms of this completely true humanity. . . .
It is not the sinlessness of a metaphysical divinity but a dynamic
sinlessness which is the free choice of his own personality.[53]

And all this comes to its completion only on the cross, where,
after a progressive stripping of his ego until the moment of
the final cry of dereliction, Jesus is utterly emptied of self,
'plunged into the *nirvana* or *suniam* where God is not', and
becomes 'the most ego-less person known in history, and
therefore the most universal of all.'[54] He did not start without
an ego or human individuality in some *aprosopic* manner: his
kenosis was achieved by the slow process of learning obedi-

[51] *Jesus the Avatar*, pp. 172f., 208. I am indebted for these and other quotations
to Boyd, op. cit., especially pp. 167–70 and 180–3.

[52] In all this, Chakkarai echoes the thought of Keshab Chandra Sen: 'Christ
ignored and denied his self altogether. . . He destroyed self. And as self ebbed away,
Heaven came pouring into the soul. For . . . nature abhors a vacuum, and hence as
soon as the soul is emptied of self, Divinity fills the void. So it was with Christ. The
Spirit of the Lord filled him, and everything was thus divine within him' (Keshub
Chunder Sen's *Lectures in India* I, p. 373). In quoting this, Boyd (op. cit., p. 29)
notes the similarity with my *Honest to God*, p. 73: 'Jesus reveals God by being
utterly transparent to him, precisely as he is nothing "in himself".' Cf. also Tillich,
Systematic Theology I, Nisbet 1953, p. 148; SCM Press 1978, p. 133.

[53] *Indian Christian Theology*, pp. 169f.

[54] *The Guardian* (Madras), 13 April 1944, quoted by P. T. Thomas, *Theology of
Chakkarai*, pp. 93–100. See also Chakkarai's earlier book, *The Cross and Indian
Thought*.

ence through the things that he suffered. Chakkarai sums it up thus:

> Jesus Christ is worshipped as God; and we cannot meet the difficulty that we are worshipping the creature instead of the Creator, unless the Christ is not a human individuality any longer. The historical Jesus was a man with an ego, and all the limitations and accidents belonging to an individual born in the world. When Jesus rose from the dead and entered the inner essence of God, then he ceased to be a human being, but became the universal spirit, though with the experience of his human history. Unique is such a state – to have the experience of humanity without the possession of an ego – which alone can give to us the Christ who while in the Being of God, the ineffable and absolute, is also an indweller, the *antaratman* [inner spirit], of those who are united with him.[55]

For, while Jesus ceases to be an individual, he remains eternally *the* avatar because his incarnation or enmanment of God is no temporary theophany restricted to a particular life but is permanent and dynamic, the firstfruits of a universal humanization of God.

I have cited this, and could have cited more, not because I should necessarily subscribe to every expression but because it is a suggestive example, from outside the logical antitheses of the Western tradition, of holding together uniqueness *and* universality, the total man, and *totus Deus*, in a way that is inclusive rather than exclusive. In this way of thinking Christ represents the focusing and concentration as in a burning glass, to use Pittenger's metaphor,[56] of all other light rather than its depreciation or denial. In words I drew upon in *The Human Face of God*, Schubert Ogden has put the matter like this:

> The claim 'only in Jesus Christ' must be interpreted to mean, not that God acts to redeem only in the history of Jesus and in no other history, but that the only God who redeems any history – *although he in fact redeems every history* – is the God whose

redemptive action is decisively represented in the word that Jesus speaks and is.[57]

And M. M. Thomas, who quotes this, adds: 'Probably this is the only form of universalism which can ultimately be called Christian.'[58]

This is still of course to make enormous claims for 'the truth as it is in Jesus' (Eph. 4.21). How may they be justified or defended? Not, I am persuaded, by saying that the historical Jesus himself had everything or was everything in an evolutionary universe. Half the proclamation of the Christ in the New Testament is after all that of the *parousia*, of the Christ who is to come, with its message: 'You ain't seen nothing yet!' Rather I believe it is by the humble witness *of those for whom it is true* that in him all things cohere and hang together (Col. 1.17) more fully than in any other such focal figure. I can only say, from my own very limited experience, that for me this is more true of Jesus as the Christ than it is of Krishna or Kali, Rama or Buddha, Moses or Mohammed, Socrates or Marx. What I need to hear from those who have lived closely with these others is what they have found of truth that can clarify, complete and correct 'the vision of Christ that I do see'.[59] Indeed, as I shall be saying in the next chapter, they are necessary to fill out my own worship and understanding as a Christian, quite apart from giving me other and complementary insights. Yet I should not be true to my apprehension of the truth if I did not also want to insist that for me the face of God as Father in the cross of Christ and the disclosure of man's destiny 'as in a son' represents the interpretation of the less than personal in experience by the personal in a manner and to a degree that I do not see anywhere else. Again I would echo the testimony of Pittenger:

For myself, I believe that the finality of Christ is nothing other than his decisive disclosure that God is suffering, saving, and

[57] *The Reality of God*, p. 173. Italics his.
[58] *The Acknowledged Christ*, p. 301.
[59] Cf. Blake, 'The Everlasting Gospel':
    The Vision of Christ that thou dost see
    Is my Vision's Greatest Enemy.

ecstatic love. Surely you cannot get anything more final than that. But there can be many different approaches to this, many different paths to its realisation, many different intimations, adumbrations, and preparations.[60]

Yet to that I would wish to add two riders. The first is that the test of inclusiveness must be how far a particular vision really does take up and transmute by incorporation rather than rejection those elements which are inimical to it. What does it make of the 'shadow' – as we instanced it earlier, for example, in the impersonal, the evil, the feminine? In these respects the Christian religion has been in its history and in many of its present manifestations a far from convincing witness to the inclusiveness of Jesus as the Christ. As we have seen, it has often been one-eyed in its understanding of God as personal, projected evil on to a devil and Antichrist, and, especially in Protestantism, subordinated the female to the image of the great white male upon the throne. But *in principle* I would still wish to claim that the Christian gospel in its central and distinctive mystery of the cross and resurrection, integrates and indeed transfigures the light and dark sides more profoundly than does the uneasy co-existence within Hinduism of Krishna and Kali; deals with the problems of suffering, and above all of sin, more dynamically and creatively than the impassive serenity of the Buddha, however moving; and incorporates the female more fully than the patriarchal religions of Judaism or (especially) Islam. On the last aspect one may comment in passing that the argument to be heard in the church today that only a male priest can represent the icon or image of Christ ignores the fact that the classical statements of Christian theology have always insisted that God became man (*anthropos*) not male (*aner*). So far from enshrining catholic tradition, it is I believe deeply heretical. Jesus indeed was a male – as a historical individual he had to be of one sex or the other, just as he had to belong to one blood-group rather than another – but in Christ there is neither male nor female, any more than there can be black or white.

---

[60] 'Christology in Process Theology', *Theology* 80, 1977, p. 193.

The second rider I should wish to add is to insist again that any uniqueness being claimed is open-ended rather than closed. Perhaps one may illustrate this by something quite central to the Christian preaching but which I have barely mentioned so far – the resurrection. Certainly I cannot embark at this stage on a treatment of it for its own sake.[61] But I have observed in inter-faith dialogue a tendency again to one-eyed extremes. Either it is argued (and this is equally true of Hindu and of Muslim approaches) that Jesus did not really die at all but that somehow (perhaps as the supreme 'yogi') he was able to exercise such control over his body that he liberated himself from the tomb by resuscitation. Or the resurrection is viewed as *the* anomalous exception, the decisive intervention by God that puts Jesus in a class by himself and 'proves' him unique. Neither of these two positions seems to me true to the New Testament. On the one hand, the resurrection, if it means anything, is clearly not the resuscitation of a man not really dead. It is not even the restoration to the old life of a corpse like Lazarus. On the other hand, the resurrection of Jesus as the Christ is never presented as an isolated exception, but as the sample and pledge of a new world. It is the promise of what ultimately must be true of the whole creation: 'As in Adam all die, so in Christ all will be brought to life' (I Cor. 15.22). Far from anticipations and partial parallels, whether for instance in the teaching of Aurobindo or in well-attested recent cases of Buddhist holy men being 'absorbed' into light,[62] being regarded as a threat, they should be welcomed as expected confirmations and illuminations. And this is fully in line, as Chakkarai pointed out,[63] with the Hindu notion of an inner or subtle body (*sukshma sarira*), a 'sheath' behind and beyond the physical body (*sthula sarira*). If Jesus was raised as 'the firstfruits of the harvest of the dead' (I Cor. 15.20), then it would be

---

[61] For fuller treatment cf. my article 'Resurrection in the New Testament', *Interpreter's Dictionary of the Bible*, Vol. IV, pp. 43–53; *The Human Face of God*, pp. 127–41; and 'The Shroud and the New Testament', in *Face to Face with the Turin Shroud*, ed. P. Jennings, ch. 5.
[62] Cf. the instances cited in *The Human Face of God*, p. 139.
[63] 'The Resurrection of our Lord', *The Guardian*, 22 April 1943, quoted by P. T. Thomas, *The Theology of Chakkarai*, pp. 69f.

strange if there were *not* 'intimations' that this was but the 'leading shoot', in Teilhard's phrase,[64] of the new humanity. Anticipating Teilhard's process of 'Christification', Keshab Chandra Sen wrote:

> The problem of creation was not how to produce one Christ, but how to make every man Christ. Christ was only a means, not the end. He was the 'way'.

> The Father continually manifests his wisdom and mercy in creation, till [men] take the form of pure sonship in Christ, and then out of one little seed-Christ is evolved a whole harvest of endless and ever-multiplying Christs.[65]

To quote Chenchiah again, whose Christology is often reminiscent of Irenaeus, with his stress on the 'recapitulation' of all men in Christ,[66] 'the Incarnation is as much about what man is to become as what God has become'.[67] 'The finality of Christ' is not a misleading phrase only if we remember that 'the perfect man' (Eph. 4.13), like 'the last Adam' (I Cor. 15.45), is a description not of the historical Jesus but of that new spiritual humanity into which mankind has yet but begun to be built. If for Christians Jesus is of 'definitive' significance, it is not because he is the last word beyond whom it is impossible to go, some static norm, like the standard metre, against which every other has for ever to be aligned, but because he offers the best clue we humans have to what Tennyson called 'the Christ that is to be'.[68] I would agree with Choan-Seng Song that 'the decisiveness of Christ'[69] is probably the least misleading term, rather than 'absoluteness', 'uniqueness' or 'finality'; and he argues along much the same lines for 'the principle of inclusiveness' as opposed to exclusivity.

Two sentences happened to strike me in an autobiography

---

[64] *The Phenomenon of Man*, p. 160.
[65] *Lectures in India* II, pp. 15, 16; quoted Boyd, *Indian Christian Theology*, p. 32.
[66] Cf. Boyd, op. cit., especially pp. 147–51.
[67] *Rethinking Christianity in India*, Appendix p. 17; quoted by Thangasamy, *Theology of Chenchiah*, p. 8.
[68] 'In Memoriam', cvi.
[69] 'The Decisiveness of Christ' in U Kyaw Than, *Asians and Blacks: Theological Challenges*. ch. 2, reprinted in *What Asian Christians are Thinking*, ed. Elwood, pp. 240–64.

which I was reading while working on this.[70] The first was: 'The belief that Christ is God-like is less important than the belief that God is Christ-like';[71] and the second: 'To believe that God is best defined by Christ is not to believe that God is confined to Christ.' Together they could sum up much of what has underlain this chapter. The first brings out that the concern for retaining some criterion among the relativities of religious claims does not stem from a competitive desire to blow up one 'bubble' over another: it comes from a common concern shared by all men of the spirit for what ultimate reality is like. And to go on to say, with the second, that this ultimate reality is Christ-like, as given definition in the person, cross and resurrection of Jesus, is not to confine the truth of God to this. It is to dare the conviction, always to be clarified, completed and corrected in dialogue, that it is this which offers the profoundest clue to all the rest.

---

[70] W. Sloane Coffin, *Once to Every Man*, pp. 116f.

[71] Cf. Chakkarai again, who spoke of the 'doctrine of the Christhood of God', *Jesus the Avatar*, p. 210.

CHAPTER VI

His Star in the East

Light from the East

There are many reasons for turning East. To me one of the
less obvious has always been why in a Christian church one
should do it to reaffirm God in the creed. Today of course
many have been doing it precisely to get away from the
Christian God, to discover what they feel they have *not* found
in the creeds. And many have found light and love, and many
disenchantment. Of that spiritual trip – and for it the East
obligingly these days comes to us – the wittiest and wisest
treatment I know is the book I referred to earlier by the
American theologian, Harvey Cox, called *Turning East*. He
is honest as to what he really got from it, especially in the
understanding and practice of meditation, and where it left
him – in many ways to his surprise a better Baptist than he
was before. Another reason for turning East, and this gets
much nearer why I found myself going there, is simply to
learn, to be stretched by truth and patterns of life of which
it is possible to remain wilfully ignorant by sitting in Cambridge – and we can no longer have the effortless superiority
to presume like J. G. Frazer that one can write *The Golden
Bough* without ever leaving Trinity Great Court! That is a
good and necessary reason for an academic to go East.

But now I want to go on to speak of why as a Christian I
felt impelled to turn East. And that could be summed up in
words which I found myself using more than once around
Epiphany-tide in South India to describe the pilgrimage on

which my wife and I were engaged: 'We have seen his star in the east and are come to worship him' (Matt. 2.2). It was not simply to understand Hinduism and Buddhism better, though that was an important objective; nor to be open to other light than that of Jesus as the Christ, though if one is humble and sensitive much comes; but, because we have seen *his* star in the East, to worship him, to shape his worth more wholly, more roundedly, than a one-eyed Western approach has allowed. We came to expand, to deepen, our vision of the truth to be found in Jesus from the light which the East sheds on him.

Now the source of this light, which illumines and points to the Christ, is not distinctively, let alone exclusively, Christian, any more than it was for the Magi whom Matthew sets at the forefront of his gospel. It was something from within their own world, drawn from the ancient wisdom of the East, whose significance they understood, but which pointed them beyond themselves till it came to rest over where the young child lay. Then they opened *their* treasures, rich and rare, to honour the king of kings.

And this has been the process, prefigured in Isa. 60.1–11, by which the nations have brought in their glory to fill out the worth of the Christ. How little would Europe have made of Christ if the understanding of him had been limited to the messianic categories of Palestinian Judaism. Beginning with Paul, and continuing through the work of men like Clement of Alexandria and Origen, the wisdom of Greece, albeit from an alien culture, was boldly drawn upon to fashion the worth of Christ for us, the children of that Western world. We think of Christianity now as being a Western religion, but this is only because it became that through men who took great risks in theology, spirituality and art, that we might know through the medium of our own cultural conditioning the wonderful works of God. But this cultural conditioning which has given us marvellous glories and shaped so rich a worth, intellectually, devotionally, architecturally, musically, and in many other ways, has become also a constriction. And it constricts not only our capacity for communicating the faith to others but now our own worship of the universal Christ. In our one

world men and women are turning East because they sense
how one-eyed we in the West have become. And instinctively
they recognize that no other country in the third world is so
rich in spiritual resources as India and the places that India
has influenced.

Now this throws a major responsibility upon the churches
of India, and upon Christians of the West in helping them,
to use and mould these resources for shaping the worth of
Christ. For it is only thus that the light from the East can
reach Europe and America through the glass of Christian
vision. Otherwise it will simply be Hindu or Buddhist wisdom, however valuable, mediated through whatever current
guru can capture the imagination or touch the pockets of the
West. Indeed, as I indicated earlier, I conceive it an important task of Christian mission today – in direct line with what
inspired Bishop Westcott and others a hundred years ago in
the founding of the Cambridge Mission to Delhi – to assist at
the birth of this new Asian theology, at the explication or
unwrapping of the mystery of Christ in Eastern terms. For
there is a wealth and depth of tradition here, spiritually,
philosophically, aesthetically, from which the entire church
catholic and ecumenical stands to benefit. Once again it
means taking risks and making mistakes, as the categories
and thought-forms, the symbolism and the art, will often be
as alien now as when the great apologists of the early church
or Aquinas in the Middle Ages wrested them from the exclusive use of the Platonists or Aristotelians.

The Christians of India as taught by their missionaries and
by what they are still hearing from the more evangelical
missions today have been on the whole cautious and defensive.[1] Indeed, as so often happens, they show themselves the
more tenacious in retaining forms from which those who
introduced them have long desired to be detached. (There

---

[1] Cf. Bishop Newbigin addressing his own flock: 'We have been too timid in
meeting with the great ideas of the world around us. We have not been willing to
get into real dialogue with Hindus, with those who are seeking new sources of vitality
for the national life, with Marxists and with humanists. We have not been willing
to take the risks involved in re-thinking our faith, re-casting it in new terms, so that
it takes up and re-interprets whatever in these movements is according to the will
of God' ('The Gospel and our Culture', in *The Good Shepherd*, p. 127).

were religious pictures, for instance, I had not seen from my childhood and which induced great nostalgia!).[2] Understandably conscious of their minority status and cultural insecurity, they have not, by and large, been positive towards the symbols of the East, innovative in their theology, original in their art[3], prophetic in their witness to the establishment. With notable and courageous exceptions their record, for instance, under Mrs Gandhi's 'emergency' was not glorious.[4] Indeed, again with splendid individual and local exceptions, it was not in the new 'pilgrim' churches from which we in the West had prepared ourselves to hope so much by reason of their unity restored, the Church of South India and the Church of North India, that one sensed the most pioneering work being done. Rather it was from the Mar Thoma church[5] (the reformed Syrian Orthodox of South India) and above all from the Roman Catholics that one learned to expect the most exciting witness.

Psychologically and sociologically one can understand this, because they have the confidence born of long roots and widespread links. With a good deal of expendable ballast (very necessary in any church) they have the freedom and the courage to be radical. But they also have a wholeness in their understanding of the gospel and a depth of spirituality which we found profoundly convincing. Indeed I had to confess to a Roman Catholic archbishop that if I stayed in India for much longer I might have to become a Roman Catholic – though fortunately I was leaving in a few days! For on the frontiers of Hindu and Buddhist dialogue and of spiritual and

[2] Yet cf. the warning of Boyd to which I was sensitive particularly in Protestant circles: 'It is a sobering fact that many of those most concerned for "Indianization" are now middle-aged and elderly, and not a few of them are foreigners!' (*Indian Christian Theology*, p. 248).

[3] But for what has been achieved in this last field, cf. Richard W. Taylor, *Jesus in Indian Paintings*, and our host in Kyoto, Masao Takenaka, *Christian Art in Asia*.

[4] The record is documented in 'Christians and the Emergency: Some Documents', *Religion and Society* 24.2 and 3, 1977.

[5] Apart from visiting their seminary at Kottyam in Kerala, appropriately on St Thomas's Day, we had regrettably little contact with them. But I have in mind the leadership of their late Metropolitan Juhanon, and of their laymen M. M. Thomas, formerly Director of the Christian Institute for the Study of Religion and Society at Bangalore, and M. A. Thomas, Director of the Ecumenical Centre at Whitefield, Bangalore.

liturgical renewal it was the Jesuits[6] and Benedictines[7] in
particular who seemed to be setting the pace. In Bangalore,
in addition to the justly renowned United Theological College
serving the Protestant denominations, I was able to see something of the impressive work of Dharmaram College for
Catholic seminarians which has been the source of a number
of important studies, including the symposium edited by J.
B. Chethimattam, *Unique and Universal,* quoted earlier, and
the quarterly *Journal of Dharma.* Also in Bangalore at the
National Biblical, Catechetical and Liturgical Centre, which
is as massive as its name, a carefully planned programme of
indigenization is being promoted from the top which would
cause a flutter in many a Protestant breast. Just as the windows of King's College Chapel, Cambridge, present a profound, if often obscure, typology of themes from the Old
Testament taken up and fulfilled in the New, so the iron
grilles in their chapel windows dare to take the Hindu symbols
and match them with their fulfilment in Christ. Their theology of mission and their *New Orders for the Mass of India*[8]
and other liturgical texts and studies are deeply thought
through, intellectually and spiritually. This is no shallow syncretism but a real baptizing into Christ of the treasures of the
East. The whole enterprise is a call, in the words of its director, Fr D. S. Amalorpavadass, 'to pass from a notion of the
Church that is sectarian and parochial, territorial and static,
introverted and imported, to a notion that is catholic and

[6] I would instance simply from our limited personal contact the symposium by
Jesuit scholars referred to earlier, *Religious Hinduism,* ed. R. De Smet and J. Neuner;
their theological seminary, Vidya Jyoti, in Delhi; the Pontifical Athenaeum, Jnana
Deepa, in Poona (which most regrettably we had to cut from an overloaded programme); the centre for inter-faith spirituality, Aikya Alayam, on the outskirts of
Madras, led by Fr Ignatius Hirudayam; and the Centre for Research and Encounter
with Buddhism near Colombo, directed by Fr Aloysius Pieris. This last works closely
with the Ecumenical Institute for Study and Dialogue (formerly The Study Centre
for Religion and Society) in Colombo directed by the Methodist Dr Lynn de Silva.

[7] The ashram at Tannirapalli near Tiruchirapally led by Dom Bede Griffiths is
focused on a chapel built in Hindu style and continues the tradition of the *Saccidananda* ashram of Monchanin and Le Saux (Abhishiktanda). For this and other
such centres, cf. Sister Vandana's survey, *Gurus, Ashrams and Christians.*

[8] Cf. their *Text for the Office of Readings,* with passages for each day from
Scripture, the Fathers, and Hindu sources. See also, among much else, D. S. Ama-
lorpavadass, *Towards Indigenization in the Liturgy,* and the report of the *Research
Seminar on Non-biblical Scriptures,* edited by him.

universal, authentic and interior, adult and dynamic.'[9]

But to avoid what would be an unbalanced and unfair picture let me throw in other examples to show that the Roman Catholics are not making all the running. One of the most encouraging things we saw was the Christian Arts and Communications Centre in Madras, which does much through the public media and the living theatre. And this was actually founded and financed by the Missouri Synod, the most conservative wing of the American Lutheran Church, many of whose members would probably be horrified to know what their money is being used for. Indeed in the Christian dances they were creating, drawing on the traditional Hindu temple dancing, they found themselves in a bind. They could not get Christian girls to take part in them, and then they could not get churches to put them on because the performers were not Christian! Moreover I would say that the most radical form of theological training I have seen anywhere, through immersing the students in workshops for the unemployed, industrial and agricultural projects and slum-living, came from the Tamil Nadu Seminary of the Church of South India at Madurai, and one of the most radical reports of the future pattern of the ministry (yet, I may say, to be implemented) from the Church of North India.[10] Yet by and large at the local level the art, the architecture, the music, even the printing, is only too often what Osbert Lancaster might have labelled 'tired missionary'. Indeed, as I took part in an Anglican service in Japan, I came to the conclusion that the only thing in the church you could not have found in the West was the slippers, with which you are carefully provided at the door of every house – a great improvement, I may say, on picking one's way barefoot through Hindu temples. Buddhism is at least a much cleaner religion, both in Ceylon and, needless to say, in Japan, where everything seems to be done, artistically and typographically,

[9] *Gospel and Culture*, p. 55. This is part of an extensive series by the same author, *Mission Theology for our Times*. He has also written a series of NBCLC Seminar Booklets, of which I would commend especially no. 1, 'Our Christian World Vision and Theological Synthesis', and no. 30, 'Inter-Religious Dialogue in India'.

[10] *A Working Document on Church Structures and Self-Reliance*, presented to the Third Synod of the CNI at Delhi, 2–6 October 1977.

with an innate sense of precision and elegance.

Indian Christian theology

But my main purpose at this point is not to offer a superficial travelogue but to draw attention to what has been and is being done in the area of Indian Christian theology. In the retrospective survey mentioned earlier, published in the *Indian Journal of Theology*,[11] Ian Clark, its recent editor until he became Chaplain of St Catharine's College, Cambridge, asked:

> Can it honestly be said that the past quarter of a century has seen the emergence of the long-awaited 'Indian Theology'? Has India contributed anything of ultimate significance in the long process of reflection and reformulation which makes up the history of Christian doctrine? Can we point to any Indian theologian who is doing for the world-Church what an Origen, an Aquinas, a Luther or a Karl Barth have done in their day? And, if anything exciting has been going on, is it reflected in the pages of *IJT*?

The answer, like its author, is modest and self-critical, though the same would surely be the result of a comparable survey, say, of the British journal *Theology*. Yet to one looking from the outside the cumulative effect is not negligible. M. M. Thomas's *The Acknowledged Christ of the Indian Renaissance* and Robin Boyd's *Introduction to Indian Christian Theology* are both impressive surveys from different angles of the dialogue that has been going on over the past hundred and fifty years between the gospel and Hindu culture. Each of these two writers has also made notable contributions of his own, Thomas on the many and various fronts we have quoted (indeed if there is a Reinhold Niebuhr of the Indian scene it is he, though as a layman in theological training he would be the first to disclaim it) and Boyd most recently in his *Khristadvaita: A Theology for India*,[12] which garners into

---

[11] 'Twenty-Four Years' Journey', *IJT* 25, 1976, p. 125.

[12] See earlier his article 'The Shape of Indian Christian Theology', *IJT* 22, 1973, pp. 15-20. He believes that this is best done in the form not of a *summa* but of a commentary (*bhasya*), like the commentaries of Shankara and Ramanuja on the *Brahma Sutra*. He builds his own theology for India (somewhat artificially at times) on the structure of the Epistle to the Romans.

a student's text-book the riches of his reading and teaching. In the breaking of fresh ground one could select two Roman Catholics, each of whom has one foot in the West and one in the East, Raymond Panikkar, whose output in several languages is prodigious, and Klaus Klostermaier, who in what is indeed a *multum in parvo* has produced in his pamphlet *Kristvidya* what he calls 'A Sketch of an Indian Christology.'[13]

It is in fact in Christology that I suspect most is to be learnt from Indian writers. For it is here above all that they find themselves with the major theological task that confronted the earliest Christian Fathers, not simply to translate the categories of Jewish messianism into those of Greek or Sanskrit, but, as Klostermaier puts it, to find 'the "theological place" of Christ within the Hindu systems as the Greek Fathers of the Church did'. For 'as long as "Christ" is just a name Christianity is just one of many sects.'[14]

'St John', he says, 'defines the essence of the *Logos* as being "*pros-ton-theon*", i.e., Christ is present wherever there is "movement towards God" (John 1.1).'[15] So *Kristvidya* must be the revelation of the hidden mystery of *Brahmavidya*, 'the highest and only aim of the Hindu theologian'. And this demands

> a full and real 'incarnation' of the Christ in the culture and categories of India – we have to find the place of Christ within the Hindu religions and systems. That it is not possible to carry him into them *from without* should be proved by now by history.[16]

He goes on:

> Greek *Christologia* did not exhaust the mystery of Christ – but it helped the Church to become aware of some aspects of it. Also Indian *Kristvidya* will not exhaust the mystery of Christ – but similarly it could help the Church to become aware of some

---

[13] The heart of it is contained in the final ch. 10 of his *Hindu and Christian in Vrindaban.*
[14] *Kristvidya*, p. 10.
[15] Op. cit., p. 17.
[16] Op. cit., p. 40.

aspects of Christ which did not come out so clearly as yet.[17]

Moreover, it could help Christians in the West as we too struggle to escape from 'the Latin captivity of the Church'. For the Greek categories of *hypostasis* filtered through the Latin *substantia* and the rest are now as much under question here as anywhere else. It has certainly been a liberation to sense even at second hand the freedom of other approaches, however tentative, which are not simply, as so often in the West, attempting to substitute for categories of physical substance those of biology or psychology but to draw upon the creative springs of inner spiritual experience (*anubhava*). For India has a tradition of immersion in Being beyond the screen of appearances which is as rich and deep as anywhere in the world and a culture where the relation between religion and philosophy has always been more vital than in either ancient Greece or modern Europe.

How the church should attempt to relate the ultimate realm of *Brahman* to the world of *maya*, whether, for instance, it should use or avoid the category of *avatar* for Christ, has divided Indian Christians as keenly as the earliest Christians were divided by whether they should take over or steer off the terminology of the Gnostics. One of the most interesting of nineteenth-century interpreters, Brahmabandhav (the equivalent of 'Theophilus') Upadhyaya sought to do justice to both positions by seeing Christ as the incarnation of *Brahman*, the divine essence, while acknowledging Krishna as an *avatara* of Vishnu, one of the personal manifestations of the Ultimate. In Boyd's summary,

> Thus Krishna is at several removes from God, and appears only in time and space, not having any existence apart from that. In other words he belongs to the realm of *maya*, of contingent being. Christ on the other hand is beyond *maya*, for he is God himself, living in the eternal dialogue of the Trinity. He too appears in history as the man Jesus, but his personality is eternally in the Godhead. Thus Krishna the *avatara* does not constitute a threat to Christ the Incarnation. In a blunt but vivid phrase Upadhyaya

[17] Op. cit., p. 41. For a brief critique of Klostermaier's Christology, cf. Samartha, *The Hindu Response*, pp. 143f.; and cf. his own following ch. 7, 'The Prerequisites of a Christology in India'.

says, 'Christ is like the sun and Krishna . . . a juicy ball!'[18]

In another attempt at expressing the same thing Panikkar
sees Christ as corresponding to *Ishvara* (Lord), 'the personal
aspect' of God,[19] rather than to *Brahman per se* or to an
avatara figure. But it has been questioned by a fellow Roman
Catholic whether he really does justice to his 'concrete and
historical humanity.'[20] Others more in *bhakti* tradition, like
Appasamy and Chakkarai, seek to present him as the true
and abiding *avatar*, of which all others are but the types and
shadows. But, whatever the particular solutions,[21] what we
witness in Indian theology is a wrestling in depth with the
great issues of the spirit which combines the mystical and
intellectual 'knowledge' (*vidya*) of the One who is beyond all
comprehension in a way that has perhaps seldom been
equalled since Chrysostom and Gregory of Nyssa.[22]

Here, for instance, is Upadhyaya's Sanskrit Hymn to the
Trinity as *Saccidananda:*

I bow to Him who is Being, Consciousness and Bliss.
I bow to Him whom worldly minds loathe,
Whom pure minds yearn for,
    The Supreme Abode.

He is the Supreme, the Ancient of days, the Transcendent,
Indivisible Plenitude, Immanent yet above all things,
Three-fold relation, pure, unrelated,
    Knowledge beyond knowledge.

The Father, Sun, Supreme Lord, unborn,
The seedless Seed of the tree of becoming,
The Cause of all, Creator, Providence,
    Lord of the universe.

---

[18] *Indian Christian Theology*, p. 82; quoting B. Animananda, *The Blade: Life
and Work of Brahmabandhav Upadhyaya*, p. 128.
[19] *The Unknown Christ of Hinduism*, pp. 119–31.
[20] Chethimattam, 'R. Panikkar's Approach to Christology', *IJT*, 23, 1974,
pp. 219–22 (221).
[21] See further Boyd, *Indian Christian Theology*, pp. 239–41, 251–4; *Khristadvaita*,
pp. 145–59; and Ryan, 'Interpreting Christ to India Today: The Contribution of the
Roman Catholic Seminaries', *IJT* 23, 1974, pp. 223–231.
[22] Cf. Otto, *The Idea of the Holy*, Appendix I. For the relevance of the Cappa-
docian Fathers to Indian Christian theology in correcting the imbalance of Western
theology, cf. Paul Verghese (now Bishop Paul Gregorios) of the Syrian Orthodox
Church, 'On God's Death: An Orthodox Contribution to the Problem of Knowing
God', *IJT* 17, 1968, pp. 151–61, and his book, *The Freedom of Man.*

The infinite and perfect Word,
The Supreme Person begotten,
Sharing in the Father's nature, Conscious by essence,
    Giver of true Salvation.

He who proceeds from Being and Consciousness,
Replete with the breath of perfect bliss,
The Purifier, the Swift, the Revealer of the Word,
    The Life-giver.

On which Boyd comments:

This is a magnificent hymn, and the deeper it is studied the more
its Christian orthodoxy stands out, despite the use of Hindu
terminology. Much of the language has Scriptural echoes, though
the vocabulary is not that of most Bible translations – Father,
Supreme Lord (*Parameshvara*), Word, begotten, Breath, Purifier, Revealer of the Word, Life-giver. Where the terminology is
derived from Hinduism – *Sat, Cit, Ananda*, 'the seedless Seed of
the tree of becoming', 'perfect bliss' – it is fully as expressive,
and indeed more vivid than the Greek or Latin-derived words
which might have been used instead. . . . Indeed it throws fresh
light on the doctrine for those who have been brought up in a
purely western theological tradition.[23]

There are others, like Chenchiah, who have started from,
and placed more stress upon, the historical Jesus and the
continuing humanity of the new man. And in the context of
Hinduism, as of ancient Gnosticism, this, as we have seen, is
bound to be a very necessary emphasis. Indeed Samartha,
whose particular contribution has been on this frontier, echoes
precisely the warnings we have given against the depreciation
of the personal, the historical, and the material:

The quest for the ground of being culminating in the *Brahman*
results in minimising the significance of the world of *history*.
Secondly, in its search for the essential nature of man culminating
in the *atman*, there is a devaluation of the human *personality*.
These two together in their mutual influence and inter-action
have contributed to the shaping of a particular outlook of clas-

[23] *Indian Christian Theology*, pp. 70f. Cf. also Upadhyaya's 'Hymn of the Incarnation', quoted ibid., pp. 77f.

sical *advaita* which has a tendency to ignore the *social* dimension of human life.[24]

One of the inbuilt correctives in Indian theology is the very fact of its long and often painful exposure to the West. It is a good deal easier for the West to be sufficient to itself. But Indian Christians have been compelled to use both eyes – their native *darshana* and the imported glass of vision. Indeed those who have served them longest and those Indians themselves who in recent times have been most exposed to the ecumenical movement and to the secularization of Asia would stress that the fullness of truth must lie in the drawing out and holding together of the three 'ways', or *margas*, present within the Hindu tradition. These are the way of knowledge (*jnana*), the way of love (*bhakti*) and the way of action (*karma*).[25] By themselves the path of *advaita*, all that Abhishiktananda sought in 'the cave of the heart', the path of devotion, espoused by Appasamy, and the path of political change, chosen by the secularizers,[26] are each in isolation inadequate.

No one perhaps has done more to hold the three in balance than M. M. Thomas, while giving his own particular emphasis to the last. 'Is there not a path', he asks, 'to understand and encounter Jesus Christ as the ground and salvation of reason and morality within a secular framework without a return to traditional religiosity?'[27] All his writings may be said to represent a wrestling with that question, not least his *Salvation and Humanisation,* another *multum in parvo*, born out of active engagement with the best of modern Western theology. In a skilful summary of his many contributions, with their characteristic emphases on 'becoming not being,' 'action not passivity,' 'love not mere unity,' Boyd closes with the words:

---

[24] *The Hindu Response*, p. 171.

[25] Panikkar treats these somewhat differently in *The Trinity and the Religious Experience of Man* as three aspects of reality which must be combined in the spirituality of the Father (*karma*), of the Son (*bhakti*), and of the Holy Spirit (*jnana*).

[26] See Thomas's most recent survey, *The Secular Ideologies of India and the Secular Meaning of Christ.*

[27] *The Acknowledged Christ*, p. 30.

All this adds up to a massive and consistent theological statement. . . . One feels that if Gandhi *had* become a Christian, and
had lived through the turmoil of the quarter century since his
death, his theology might have been something like this.[28]

Thomas's friend and colleague at Bangalore, Russell Chandran, Principal of the United Theological College, who has
also himself been the subject of a very impressive recent
Festschrift,[29] concludes a 'critical survey' of the 'Development
of Christian Theology in India'[30] with a similar plea for the
holding together of 'two poles':

> True theology is not just a process of formulation of doctrines,
> but a process of doing, a process of participating in the real
> presence of Christ with two poles, one the sacramental partici-
> pation and the other a contemporary re-enactment of the exodus-
> covenant experience for people suffering from different forms of
> oppression. It is when this dimension becomes the real basis of
> Indian theology, grappling with the totality of the Indian reli-
> gious, social and cultural situation in which the Indian humanity
> is caught up, that Indian Christian theology will share in the
> universal concern of Christian theology.

There is still a future tense in that last sentence, as there
would have to be in an honest statement of any other regional
theology. But it points to a yearning within Indian Christian
theology itself for a 'two-eyed' vision of truth and praxis, with

[28] *Indian Christian Theology*, p. 330. See ch. 16 as a whole.
[29] *A Vision for Man*, ed. S. Amirtham. Unfortunately I received it too late to be
able to integrate its contributions into the body of the text, but I would draw
attention to the following as especially significant for the themes of this book: A. P.
Nirmal, 'Towards a Relevant and Contemporary Theology in India' (pp. 61–77),
which argues cogently for a Christian 'middle way' between *advaita vedanta* and
the ancient but largely forgotten tradition of Indian materialism and empiricism
known as *lakayata* and which is particularly relevant to the theme of ch. 4; S.
Amirtham on the rationale of the Tamil Nadu Seminary at Madurai (see p. 135
above), of which he is Principal (pp. 143–51); P. B. Santram, the Principal of
Bishop's College, Calcutta, on indigenization, including a valuable bibliography of
the issue (pp. 180–99); Choan-Seng Song, whose radical missionary theology was
referred to earlier (pp. 117f.), on the total mission of God (pp. 221–37); A. D. John
General Secretary of the Christian Literature Society, Madras, deploring the insu-
larity of Indian Christians (pp. 238–52); three useful essays on recent developments
in dialogue by Lukas Vischer, S. Wesley Ariarajah and T. Dayananda Francis
(pp. 252–81); and Dyanchand Carr, 'Jesus and the World Religions' (pp. 282–302),
a reply to Hick's essay in *The Myth of God Incarnate*, which is very relevant to
ch. 5.
[30] *Bangalore Theological Forum* 8, 1976, pp. 138–55 (155).

the same combining of the mystical and prophetic, the 'unitive' and 'communitive', for which we have been pleading. None of us, whether from East or West, will achieve this in what has hitherto been far too much of an unhealthy isolation. We need each other.

There are, of course, many other partial visions to be brought together, many other 'eyes' on truth. But let me close with two characteristic quotations from Chenchiah, reflecting upon the peculiar contribution of India to Christian theology:

> Even if a common faith could be evolved without her, it cannot be completed without her contribution;[31]

and

> The negative plate of Jesus, developed in a solution of Hinduism, brings out hitherto unknown features of the portrait and these may prove exactly the 'Gospel' for our time.[32]

[31] *The Guardian*, 30 January 1947; quoted Boyd, *The Latin Captivity*, p. 144.
[32] *Rethinking Christianity in India*, p. 162; quoted Boyd, *Indian Christian Theology*, p. 164.

Some Addresses

One of the problems, as I found, for anyone wishing to keep in touch with what is happening in Indian theology is simply the difficulty of access to materials. (It was not lessened for me when a large package of books posted back from India never arrived, but that is one of the natural hazards.) Much too little is published directly in the West.

A useful source-book, full of well-documented information, is W. Owen Cole, (ed.) *World Religions: A Handbook for Teachers*, published by the Commission for Racial Equality, Elliott House, 10–12 Allington Street, London SW1E 5EH. Apart, for instance, from 'Fifty Books on Hinduism' it has, most commendably, two pages (111–13) of titles on Indian Christian Theology selected by Eric Sharpe.

The following are sources of contact for many of the books and periodicals I have referred to:

1. *In India:*

The Christian Institute for the Study of Religion and Society (CISRS – locally known as 'Scissors'), PO Box 4600, Bangalore, 560 046. It produces *Religion and Society* quarterly and has a notable record in stimulating some of the best material on the frontiers between Christian theology, politics and other religions. Its 'library subscription' (currently £8 per annum), covering *Religion and Society* and every CISRS publication during the year, is described by Sharpe as 'undoubtedly the "best buy" in religious literature today.'

The Christian Literature Society (CLS), PO Box 501, Park Town, Madras, 600 003, publishes most of the CISRS productions and much else. Almost all the books of recent years I have listed as published in Madras come from this press.

The Indian Society for the Promotion of Christian Knowledge (ISPCK), PO Box 1585, Kashmere Gate, Delhi, 110 006.

The National Biblical, Catechetical and Liturgical Centre (NBCLC), PO Bag 577, Bangalore, 560 005.

Dharmaram Publications, Dharmaram College, Bangalore, 560 029.

Theological Publications in India (TPI), St Peter's Seminary, Bangalore, 560 012.

Vidya Jyoti, Institute of Religious Studies, 23 Raj Niwas Marg, Delhi, 110 054.

Jnana Deepa, Institute of Philosophy and Religion, Pune (Poona), 411 014.

The Indian Journal of Theology (IJT), Bishop's College, 224 Acharya Jagadish Bose Road, Calcutta, 700 017.

The Ecumenical Institute for Study and Dialogue, 490–5 Havelock Road, Colombo 6, Sri Lanka.

Christian ashrams and dialogue centres in India are listed in Sister Vandana's *Gurus, Ashrams and Christians*, pp. 113–5, published by Darton, Longman & Todd, 89 Lillie Road, London, SW6 1UD.

2. *In Britain:*

The United Society for Christian Literature (USCL) acts as agent for CLS of Madras. Catalogue and books are obtainable from the Lutterworth Press, Luke House, Farnham Road, Guildford, Surrey.

The Society for the Promotion of Christian Knowledge (SPCK) acts as agent for ISPCK, Delhi. Catalogue and books from Holy Trinity Church, Marylebone Road, London NW1 4DU.

Third World Publications Ltd., 151 Stratford Road, Birmingham B11 1RD, publishes a list of Third World Christian Books (including R. H. S. Boyd's *Introduction to Indian Christian Theology*). In London these books may be obtained from the Tavistock Bookshop, 86 Tavistock Place, WC1, or from the Methodist Bookshop, 25 Marylebone Road, NW1.

The Student Christian Movement (SCM) Bookroom, 56 Bloomsbury Street, London WC1B 3QX, publishes an annual book-guide, *Religion and Theology*, which has a section on World Religions. It includes M. M. Thomas's *The Acknowledged Christ of the Indian Renaissance*.

Libraries: The Selly Oak Colleges, Birmingham B29 6LE; The Church Missionary Society (CMS), 157 Waterloo Road, London SE1 8UU; Heythrop College, 11–13 Cavendish Square, London W.1.

3. *In Rome:*

Centre for Indian and Inter-Religious Studies, Via Martini V 26/B, 00167 Roma, Italy.

Bibliography

of works cited in the text

(Unless otherwise stated the place of publication is London.)

Abhishiktananda, Swami, *Hindu-Christian Meeting Point*, Bangalore and Bombay 1969, Delhi ²1976
— *Guru and Disciple*, SPCK 1974
— *The Further Shore*, Delhi 1975
— *Saccidananda: A Christian Approach to Advaitic Experience*, Delhi 1974
— *Swami Param Arubi Anandam: Memoir of Jules Monchanin*, Tiruchirapalli 1959
Akhilananda, Swami, *The Hindu View of Christ*, Philosophical Library, New York 1949
Amalorpavadass, D. S., *Gospel and Culture*, Bangalore 1978
— *Towards Indigenization in the Liturgy*, 1971
— (ed.), *Research Seminar on Non-Biblical Scriptures*, Bangalore 1975
Amirtham, S. (ed.), *A Vision for Man* , Madras 1978
Anderson, Norman, *The Mystery of the Incarnation*, Hodder & Stoughton 1978
Animananda, B., *The Blade: Life and Work of Brahmabandhav Upadhyaya*, Calcutta 1947
Appasamy, A. J., *Christianity as Bhaktimarga*, Madras 1926; Macmillan 1927
— *The Gospel and India's Heritage*, SPCK and Madras 1942
— *My Theological Quest*, Madras 1964
— *Temple Bells*, SCM Press 1930
— *What is Moksha? A Study in the Johannine Doctrine of Life*, Madras 1931
Arberry, A. J., *Sufism*, Allen & Unwin 1930

Aurobindo, Sri, *The Upanishads*, Birth Centenary Library XII, Pondicherry 1972
— *Essays on the Gita*, Birth Centenary Library XIII, Pondicherry 1970
— *The Supernatural Manifestation*, Birth Centenary Library XVI, Pondicherry 1971

Barbour, I. G., *Issues in Science and Religion*, SCM Press and Prentice-Hall, Englefield Cliffs, NJ, 1966
Barth, Karl, *The Humanity of God*, ET John Knox Press, Philadelphia 1960, Collins 1961
Beckett, L. C., *Neti-Neti*, J. M. Watkins [2]1959
Benedict, Ruth, *The Chrysanthemum and the Sword*, Secker & Warburg 1947; New American Library, New York 1967
Benz, E., *Buddhism or Communism*, ET Allen & Unwin and Doubleday, New York 1966
Berdyaev, N., *Freedom and the Spirit*, Geoffrey Bles and Scribner's, New York 1935
— *Spirit and Reality*, Geoffrey Bles and Scribner's 1939
Bonhoeffer, Dietrich, *Christology*, Collins and Harper & Row, New York 1971
— *Letters and Papers from Prison*, The Enlarged Edition, SCM Press and Macmillan, New York 1971
Boyd, R. H. S., *An Introduction to Indian Christian Theology*, Madras [1]1969, [2]1975
— *India and the Latin Captivity of the Church: The Cultural Context of the Gospel*, Cambridge University Press and Scottish Academic Press, Edinburgh 1974
— *Khristadvaita: A Theology for India*, Madras 1977
Braybrooke, Marcus, *The Undiscovered Christ*, Madras 1973
Brunner, Emil, *Man in Revolt*, ET Lutterworth Press and Scribner's 1939
Bruns, J. Edgar, *The Christian Buddhism of St John*, Paulist Press, New York 1971
Buber, Martin, *I and Thou*, ET R. Gregor Smith, T. and T. Clark and Scribner's 1937; ET W. Kaufmann, T. and T. Clark and Scribner's 1970
— *Between Man and Man*, ET Routledge & Kegan Paul 1947, Macmillan, New York 1948

Capra, F., *The Tao of Physics*, Fontana 1976, Bantam Books, New York 1977
Carman, J. B., *The Theology of Ramanuja*, Yale University Press 1974

Chakkarai, Vengal, *Jesus the Avatar*, Madras 1926
— *The Cross and Indian Thought*, Madras 1932
Chethimattam, J. B., *Dialogue in Indian Tradition*, Bangalore 1969
— *Patterns of Indian Thought*, Geoffrey Chapman 1971
— (ed.), *Unique and Universal*, Bangalore 1972
Choan-Seng Song, *Christian Mission in Reconstruction – an Asian Attempt*, Madras 1975
Coffin, W. Sloane, *Once to Every Man*, Athenaeum Publishers, New York 1977
Coomaraswamy, A. K., *The Dance of Siva*, Noonday Press, New York 1957, Peter Owen 1958
Cox, Harvey, *The Secular City*, Macmillan, New York and SCM Press 1965
— *Turning East: The Promise and the Peril of the New Orientalism*, Simon & Schuster, New York 1977
Cross, F. L. (ed.), *The Oxford Dictionary of the Christian Church*, Oxford University Press ¹1957, ²1974

Dasgupta, S. N., *Hindu Mysticism*, Open Court, Chicago 1927
Davis, Charles, *Body as Spirit: The Nature of Religious Feeling*, Hodder & Stoughton and Seabury Press, New York 1976
— *Christ and the World Religions*, Hodder & Stoughton 1970
Devanandan, P. D., *Christian Concern in Hinduism*, Bangalore 1961
— *The Concept of Maya*, Lutterworth Press 1950
— *Preparation for Dialogue*, Madras 1967
Dhavamony, M., *Love of God according to the Saiva Siddhanta: A Study in the Mysticism and Theology of Saivism*, Oxford University Press 1971
Dillistone, F. W., *C. H. Dodd: Interpreter of the New Testament*, Hodder & Stoughton and Eerdmans, Grand Rapids, Mich. 1977
Dodd, C. H., *The Interpretation of the Fourth Gospel*, Cambridge University Press 1953
— *More New Testament Studies*, Manchester University Press 1968
Dumitriu, Petru, *Incognito*, ET Collins and Macmillan, New York 1964
Dunne, John S., *The Way of All the Earth*, Sheldon Press and Macmillan, New York 1972
Duraisingh, C., and Hargreaves, C., *India's Search for Reality and the Relevance of the Gospel of St John*, Delhi 1975
Dutt, R. Palme, *India Today*, Gollancz and Ryerson Press, Toronto 1940

Eliot, T. S., *Four Quartets*, Harcourt Brace, New York 1943, Faber 1944

Elwood, D. J. (ed.), *What Asian Christians are Thinking: A Theological Source Book*, New Day Publishers, Quezon City, Philippines 1976

Farmer, H. H., *Revelation and Religion*, Nisbet and Harper & Bros., New York 1954

Forster, E. M., *Passage to India*, pocket edition, Edward Arnold and Longmans, Toronto 1947

Gandhi, Mahatma, *The Message of Jesus Christ*, Bombay 1940

Gispert-Sauch, G. (ed.), *God's Word among Men*, Delhi 1973

Graham, Aelred, *The End of Religion: Autobiographical Explorations*, Harcourt Brace Jovanovich, New York 1971

Green, Michael (ed.), *The Truth of God Incarnate*, Hodder & Stoughton 1977

Griffiths, Bede, *Christian Ashram: Essays towards a Hindu-Christian Dialogue*, Darton, Longman & Todd 1966

— *Return to the Centre*, Collins and Templegate, Springfield, Ill. 1976

— *Vedanta and Christian Faith*, Dawn Horse Press, San Francisco 1973

Happold, F. C., *Religious Faith and Twentieth-Century Man*, Penguin 1966

Healey, F. G. (ed.), *Prospect for Theology: Essays in Honour of H. H. Farmer*, Nisbet 1966

Heiler, F., *Prayer*, ET Oxford University Press 1932

Hesse, Hermann, *Siddhartha*, ET New Directions, New York 1951, Peter Owen 1954

Hick, John, *Christianity at the Centre*, SCM Press and Allenson, Naperville 1969, subsequently republished as *The Centre of Christianity*, SCM Press and Harper & Row, New York 1977

— (ed.,), *The Myth of God Incarnate*, SCM Press and Westminster Press, Philadelphia 1977

Hiriyanna, M., *Outlines of Indian Philosophy*, Allen & Unwin and Macmillan, New York 1932

Hooker, Roger, *Outside the Camp*, Madras and Delhi 1972, republished as *Uncharted Journey*, CMS 1973

— *Journey into Varanasi*, CMS 1978

Hume, R. E. (trans.), *The Thirteen Principal Upanishads*, Oxford University Press ²1931

Jennings, Peter (ed.), *Face to Face with the Turin Shroud*, Mayhew-McCrimmon and Mowbray 1978

Jeremias, Joachim, *The Prayers of Jesus*, ET SCM Press 1967, Fortress Press, Philadelphia 1977

Jones, E. Stanley, *Mahatma Gandhi, an Interpretation*, Hodder & Stoughton and Abingdon Press 1948

Jung, C. G., *Aion*, Collected Works IX.2, Routledge & Kegan Paul and Pantheon Books, New York 1959

— *Answer to Job*, Collected Works XI, Routledge & Kegan Paul and Pantheon Books ²1969

— *Memories, Dreams, Reflections*, ET Collins and Pantheon Books 1963

Käsemann, Ernst, *The Testament of Jesus*, ET SCM Press and Fortress Press, Philadelphia 1968

King, Ursula M., *Towards a New Mysticism: Teilhard de Chardin and Eastern Religions*, Collins 1980

Kinsley, David R., *The Sword and the Flute*, University of California Press 1975

Klostermaier, Klaus, *Hindu and Christian in Vrindaban*, SCM Press 1969

— *Kristvidya*, Bangalore 1967

Koyama, Kosuke, *No Handle on the Cross*, SCM Press and Orbis Books, New York 1976

—*Waterbuffalo Theology*, SCM Press and Orbis Books, New York 1974

Kraemer, H., *The Christian Message in a Non-Christian World*, Edinburgh House Press and Harper & Bros., New York 1938

Kroll, Una, *Lament for a Lost Enemy*, SPCK 1977

— *TM, A Signpost for the World: An Assessment of Transcendental Meditation*, Darton, Longman and Todd 1974

Lampe, G. W. H., *God as Spirit*, Oxford University Press 1977

Lindars, Barnabas, and Smalley, Stephen S. (eds.), *Christ and Spirit in the New Testament*, Cambridge University Press 1973

Ling, T. O., *Buddhism and the Mythology of Evil: A Study in Theravada Buddhism*, Allen and Unwin 1962

Lubac, H. de, *The Faith of Teilhard de Chardin*, ET Burns and Oates 1965 = *Teilhard de Chardin: the Man and his Meaning*, Hawthorn Books, New York 1965

Mackey, James M., *Jesus: the Man and the Myth*, SCM Press and Paulist Press, New York 1979

McDermott, Robert A., ed., *Six Pillars: Introductions to the Major*

Works of Sri Aurobindo, Conococheagne Associates, Chambersburg, Pa. 1974

Mascall, E. L., *Theology and the Gospel of Christ*, SPCK 1977

Merton, Thomas, *Asian Journal*, Sheldon Press 1974

Minz, Nirmal, *Mahatma Gandhi and Hindu-Christian Dialogue*, Madras 1970

Miranda, José P., *Marx and the Bible*, ET Orbis Books, Maryknoll 1974, SCM Press 1977

Monod, Jacques, *Chance and Necessity*, ET Knopf, New York 1971, Collins 1972

Moule, C. F. D., *The Origin of Christology*, Cambridge University Press 1977

Muller, Max, *Ramakrishna: His Life and Sayings*, Collected Works XV, Longmans 1900

Neill, Stephen C., *Bhakti Hindu and Christian*, Madras 1974

Newbigin, Lesslie, *A Faith for this One World?* SCM Press and Allenson, Naperville 1961; Epworth Press 1965

— *The Finality of Christ*, SCM Press 1969

— *The Good Shepherd: Meditations on Christian Ministry in Today's World*, Madras 1974

Niebuhr, Reinhold, *The Nature and Destiny of Man*, Scribner's, New York and Nisbet 1941–43

Nikhilananda, Swami, *Western Mechanism and Hindu Mysticism*, Ramakrishna Mission Institute of Culture, Calcutta 1940

— (ed.), *The Upanishads*, Phoenix House 1951

Norman, Edward R., *Christianity and World Order*, Oxford University Press 1979

O'Flaherty, Wendy D., *Asceticism and Eroticism in the Mythology of Siva*, Oxford University Press 1973

— *The Origins of Evil in Hindu Mythology*, University of California Press, 1976

Ogden, Schubert M., *The Reality of God*, SCM Press and Harper & Row, New York 1967

Otto, Rudolf, *The Idea of the Holy*, ET Oxford University Press 1926

— *India's Religion of Grace*, ET SCM Press and Macmillan, New York 1930

— *Mysticism East and West*, ET Macmillan 1932

Panikkar, K. M., *Foundations of the New India*, Allen & Unwin 1963, Humanities Press, New York 1964

Panikkar, R., *The Trinity and the Religious Experience of Man*,

ET Darton, Longman & Todd and Orbis Books, New York 1973
— *The Unknown Christ of Hinduism*, Darton, Longman & Todd 1964, Humanities Press, New York 1968
— *The Vedic Experience*, Darton, Longman & Todd and University of California Press 1977
Pannenberg, W., *Basic Questions in Theology* I, ET SCM Press and Fortress Press, Philadelphia 1970
Parrinder, Geoffrey, *Avatar and Incarnation*, Faber 1970
— *Mysticism in the World's Religions*, Oxford University Press 1977
Peacocke, A. R., *Creation and the World of Science*, Oxford University Press 1979

Radhakrishnan, S., *Eastern Religions and Western Thought*, Oxford University Press 1939, ²1940
— *The Hindu View of Life*, Allen & Unwin and Macmillan, New York 1927
— *Indian Philosophy*, Allen & Unwin and Macmillan, New York ²1929
— *Religion and Society*, Allen & Unwin and Macmillan, New York 1947
— *Religion in a Changing World*, Allen & Unwin and Harper & Row, New York 1967
— *(ed.), Bhagavadgita*, Allen & Unwin and Harper & Bros. 1948
— *Brahma Sutra*, Allen & Unwin and Harper & Row 1960
— *The Principal Upanishads*, Allen & Unwin and Harper & Bros. 1953
Radhakrishnan, S., and Muirhead, J. H., (eds.), *Contemporary Indian Philosophy*, Allen & Unwin and Macmillan, New York ¹1936, ²1952
Rao, Mark Sunder, *Ananyatva: Realization of Christian Non-Duality*, Bangalore 1974
'Rethinking' Group (Chenchiah, Chakkarai, etc.), *Rethinking Christianity in India*, Madras 1938
Rice, Cyprian, *The Persian Sufis*, Allen & Unwin and Hillary House, New York 1964
Robinson, John A. T., *But That I Can't Believe!*, Fontana Books and New American Library, New York 1967
— *Exploration into God*, Stanford University Press and SCM Press 1967, reissued Mowbrays 1977
— *Honest to God*, SCM Press and Westminster Press, Philadelphia 1963
— *The Human Face of God*, SCM Press and Westminster Press 1973

— *Liturgy Coming to Life*, Mowbrays 1960
— *On Being the Church in the World*, SCM Press 1960, Westminster Press 1962, reissued Mowbrays 1977
— *Redating the New Testament*, SCM Press and Westminster Press 1976

Saint-Hilaire, P. B., *The Future Evolution of Man: The Life Divine upon Earth*, Pondicherry 1963
Samartha, S. J., *The Hindu Response to the Unbound Christ*, Madras 1974
— *The Hindu View of History, Classical and Modern*, Bangalore 1959
— *Introduction to Radhakrishnan*, Association Press, New York 1964
Sangharakshita, Bhikshu, *The Three Jewels*, Rider 1967
Schlipp, P. A. (ed.), *The Philosophy of Sarvepalli Radhakrishnan*, Cambridge University Press and Tudor Publishing Co., New York 1952
Schoonenberg, Piet, *The Christ*, ET Seabury Press, New York 1971, Sheed and Ward 1972
Schumacher, E. F., *Small is Beautiful*, Harper & Row, New York 1973, Abacus Books 1974
Schweitzer, A., *Indian Thought and Its Development*, Hodder & Stoughton and Holt, New York 1936
Sen, Keshub Chunder, *The Brahmo Somaj, Lectures in India*, Cassell 1901–04
Sharpe, E. J., *Faith Meets Faith*, SCM Press 1977
Silva, L. A. de, *Buddhism: Beliefs and Practices in Sri Lanka*, Colombo 1974
— *The Problem of the Self in Buddhism and Christianity*, Colombo 1975, ²Macmillan 1979
Singh, H. Jai (ed.), *Inter-Religious Dialogue*, Bangalore 1967
Singh, Maharaj Charan, *St John the Great Mystic*, Radhasoami Satsang, Beas, Punjab ¹1967, ²1971
Smet, R. De and Neuner, J. (eds.), *Religious Hinduism*, St Paul's Publications, Allahabad ¹1964, ²1968
Smith, W. Cantwell, *The Meaning and End of Religion*, Macmillan, New York 1962
Smart, Ninian, *The Yogi and the Devotee*, Allen & Unwin and Humanities Press, New York 1968
Suzuki, D. T., *Mysticism, Christian and Buddhist*, Allen & Unwin and Harper & Bros., New York 1957
Sykes, S. W. and Clayton, J.P. (eds.), *Christ, Faith and History*, Cambridge University Press 1972

Takenaka, Masao, *Christian Art in Asia*, Tokyo 1975

Tawney, R. H., *Religion and the Rise of Capitalism*, John Murray and Harcourt Brace, New York, 1926

Taylor, Richard W., *Jesus in Indian Paintings*, Madras 1975

— (ed.), *Society and Religion*, Madras 1976

Teilhard de Chardin, Pierre, *The Activation of Energy*, Collins 1970, Harcourt Brace Jovanovich, New York 1971

— *Christianity and Evolution*, Collins and Harcourt Brace Jovanovich 1971

— *The Heart of Matter*, Collins and Harcourt Brace Jovanovich 1978

— *Hymn of the Universe*, Collins and Harper & Row, New York 1965

— *Le Milieu Divin*, Collins 1960 = *Divine Milieu*, Harper & Row 1960

— *The Phenomenon of Man*, Collins and Harper & Bros., New York 1959

— *Writings in Time of War*, Collins and Harper & Row 1968

Temple, William, *Nature, Man and God*, Macmillan 1934

— *What Christians Stand for in the Secular World*, Supplement to the Christian Newsletter, 29 December 1943

Tenzin Gyatsho, *The Opening of the Wisdom Eye*, Adyar, Madras 1971

Thangasamy, D. A., *The Theology of Chenchiah*, Madras 1966

Thomas, M. M., *The Acknowledged Christ of the Indian Renaissance*, SCM Press 1969

— *The Christian Response to the Asian Revolution*, SCM Press 1966

— *Man and the Universe of Faiths*, Madras 1975

— *Salvation and Humanisation*, Madras 1971

— *The Secular Ideologies of India and the Secular Meaning of Christ*, Madras 1976

Thomas, P. T., *The Theology of Chakkarai*, Madras 1968

Tillich, Paul, *Christianity and the Encounter of the World Religions*, Columbia University Press 1963

— *The Courage to Be*, Yale University Press 1952, Nisbet 1953

— *Systematic Theology* I–III, Nisbet 1953–64; University of Chicago Press 1951–63, reissued SCM Press 1978

U Kyaw Than, *Asians and Blacks: Theological Challenges*, East Asia Christian Council, Bangkok 1973

Vandana, Sister, *Gurus, Ashrams and Christians*, Darton, Longman and Todd 1978

Verghese, Paul, *The Freedom of Man*, Westminster Press, Philadelphia 1972

Vivekananda, Swami, *Complete Works*, Mayavati Memorial Edition, Calcutta 1955–62

Watts, Alan W., *Behold the Spirit* (1947), Random House, New York ²1972

— *Beyond Theology*, Pantheon Books, New York 1964, Hodder & Stoughton 1966

— *The Two Hands of God: The Myths of Polarity* (1963), Macmillan, New York 1969

— *The Way of Zen*, Pantheon Books, New York 1957; Penguin Books 1962

Webb, C. C. J., *God and Personality*, Allen & Unwin and Macmillan, New York 1918

Whitson, R. E., *The Coming Convergence of World Religions*, Newman Press, New York 1971

Wood, Barry, *The Magnificent Frolic*, Westminster Press, Philadelphia 1970

Younger, Paul, *Introduction to Indian Religious Thought*, Darton, Longman and Todd and Westminster Press, Philadelphia 1972

Zaehner, R. C., *Evolution in Religion*, Oxford University Press 1971

— *Hinduism*, Oxford University Press 1962

— *Hindu Scriptures*, Everyman Library, Dent and Dutton, New York 1966

— *Mysticism, Sacred and Profane*, Oxford University Press 1972

— (ed.), *The Bhagavad-Gita, with a Commentary based on the Original Sources*, Oxford University Press 1969.

Zahrnt, Heinz, *The Historical Jesus*, ET Collins and Harper & Row, New York 1963

New Directions in Faith and Order, World Council of Churches, Geneva 1966

New Orders for the Mass of India, NBCLC, Bangalore 1974

Text for the Office of Readings, NBCLC, Bangalore 1973–74

Index of Names